Just Fishing Talk

The Sawkill from an Old Steel Engraving

JUST
FISHING TALK

GIFFORD PINCHOT

Author of
"To the South Seas"

Illustrated with Photographs

STACKPOLE
BOOKS
Lanham • Boulder • New York • London

Published by Stackpole Books
An imprint of The Rowman & Littlefield Publishing Group, Inc.
4501 Forbes Boulevard, Suite 200, Lanham, Maryland 20706
www.rowman.com

Unit A, Whitacre Mews, 26-34 Stannary Street, London SE11 4AB

Distributed by NATIONAL BOOK NETWORK

British Library Cataloguing in Publication Information Available

ISBN 978-0-8117-3688-6 (paperback)
ISBN 978-0-8117-6654-8 (electronic)

♾ The paper used in this publication meets the minimum requirements of
American National Standard for Information Sciences—Permanence of Paper
for Printed Library Materials, ANSI/NISO Z39.48-1992.

Printed in the United States of America

CONTENTS

PREFACE

You love to fish, and so do I. You love the great out-doors, and that's another thing we have in common. All right—let's have some fishing talk.

Here's my contribution. I hope I'll have the luck to hear yours some day.

Fish stories improve with age. Some of these veracious tales were written so many light-years ago and have remained uncontradicted so long that you are obliged, out of sheer courtesy, to believe them. I believe them myself.

Some of them deal with little rivers and quiet waters, some with the open sea. The fish they tell of run from ounces to tons. I've had great sport with all—as much with the small as with the great. And now I'd like to share that sport with you.

If I've described more than one episode as the very best fishing I ever had, don't let that disturb you. It *was* the very best, or seemed so at the time. I'm trying to make you see and feel as I saw and felt myself. Besides, as to any fish story whatsoever, the higher criticism is out of place.

Several of these stories have previously been published in AMERICAN ANGLER, COLLIER'S, FIELD AND STREAM, OUT-DOOR AMERICA, ROTARIAN, and the SATURDAY EVENING POST. *Sea Bat and Whale Iron* and *Tree-Climbing Angle Worms* appeared first in the author's TO THE SOUTH SEAS published by the John C. Winston Co. and later reprinted in a Blue Ribbon Book.

G. P.

Yesterday

YESTERDAY was cool. It looked like rain, and the wind was in the East. Where I live a gentle Southwest wind is the wind for trout, and the hotter the better —that is for trout by the dry fly route. For then the living flies are out in their millions. May-flies, Stone-flies, Caddis-flies, and all the host of daylight- and twilight-loving winged triflers with death, swing and float and flash and dip and hover, in their seasons, over the hungry mouths beneath; and the trout wax portly, yet are never satisfied.

But when the wind is in the East, although insects swarm and food offers itself in plenty, the trout you shall catch shall be gaunt and empty, and in Pike County at least, they will be few and far between.

Which brings me back to yesterday, when the wind was in the East, and it was cold. The day before was warmer and before that it was hot. On such a day as yesterday fishing should have been at its worst. Yet the day was cloudy. In the afternoon rain threatened. At last a drop or two fell upon my desiccated hopes of fishing, which being thus watered began again to flourish and grow green.

I know a place where rain at sunset brings the big ones to the table—first to their table and then to mine. The thought of it made me uneasy, began to bite in, grew irresistible. 'Tis better to have fished and lost than never to have fished at all.

Hastily I collected my boots and my creel, the little tin box that used to hold Bulgarian bacilli and now holds Malloch flies, the rod Rubia gave me, and the little rattan landing net with the broken meshes. The flivver was ready and I started—almost. For here came a youngster demanding to know where I was going and what I would do when I got there, and before I could make an answer that would pass, here came another demanding to go wherever it was, and the two combined to require and insist that Rubia must go also. But Rubia declined.

So I compromised on a run to the village on the excuse of finding a fishing partner (who wouldn't go anyway because of the rain). Down we went and back we came, my live freight was delivered safe again at home, and up over the hill and through the wood I reached the brookside just as the rain came down in earnest on top of my old straw hat, through which it seemed to pass without even hesitating.

In the old beaver meadow there wasn't a rise in sight. Two fish were feeding on a shallow on some under-water prey, but a dry fly in the rain had no charms for them. Repeatedly I dropped my pale evening dun just ahead of their arrowy wakes. Repeatedly they passed beneath it and scorned it as they passed. I was reflecting that they might be stray pickerel anyhow, and that they were a long way off at best, when there came a smashing rise some fifty yards above.

For that fellow what skill I had I made full use of— kept far back and low down, cast only the leader beyond the long stiff grass, and even broke away and lost a fly caught on a stub of willow, and tied on its successor and presented it without moving from my place and position. Which meant more than you might think, for the wind had fallen, and the midges were out in swarms, thick enough and eager enough to double the time and quadruple the irritation of that delicate proceeding.

Happy Days Will Come Again

But that trout knew more about fishing than I did, and would not even come and look at the best I had to show. So I left him for another fish that was breaking the surface just above me, and for him I changed my fly to a Coachman of the smallest size. Fine and far I cast to him and in divers ways did the prettiest I knew, as I had often done before beside those quiet waters, and for my pains got nothing but the pleasure of the casting and the beauty of the time and the place.

These failures made every mosquito more annoying, every gnat more poisonous, and every rain drop colder as it drove through my hat. Evidently it was time to move away from there, to the head of the great pool where the big ones come when the rain reminds them of what the stream is going to bring down. More than half the margin of the great pool is screened with alders, so that you cannot altogether choose your ground. But at the head is an open space and in it an old log, mostly under water, from which a careful fisherman may reach across and down the entering current.

Trout were rising in the swift water, and here and there one in the pool, in their regular places. It is the most natural of all things, but worth recalling, that some positions even in the body of a pool are better than others from the point of view of a hungry trout, and that not all such places are at the beginning or at the end of the quiet water.

Some of these places were beyond my reach, for I was fishing with the rod I allow myself to use only on special occasions, the little seven foot 2⅜ oz. rod Leonard built to exhibit at the San Francisco Exposition, and in the calm judgment of its unprejudiced owner the best rod—the very best rod—that has yet been produced in this otherwise imperfect world. Moreover, Rubia gave it to me, as I remarked before.

All of which being admitted, I return to the head of the pool from which the little rod, in spite of its marvelous casting power, did not enable me to cover all the rising fish.

But I didn't need to. The second cast in the ripple brought a sharp response, and a lively little fight ended with a half pound native trout in the net. Then came a brown, about half as heavy again, and another native. It was the best kind of good fishing, at least for Pike County in the Year of Grace 1920.

The swift water comes into the great pool through a long straight reach of rapid water lined with dense brush and overhung with trees. It is no easy place to fish without losing flies and leaders, for all it looks so straight. Tonight there was a rising fish close to the bank, well above the pool, hard to reach (without disturbing the water) for one of the army of moderate casters like myself, who write so few fish stories but do so much fishing.

At last, however, my hand was fortunate. The fly lit gently just above the rise, and a foot or two farther out. There was a lazy sucking of it in, and then like a flash of light my line went past me as the trout shot down the current to the center of the pool—down, and back, and across, (luckily turned and only just turned at the fringe of the alders), up to the head again, and to the bottom among the stones. The leader was light in due proportion to the rod, and the tiny fly required delicate handling. The reel sang again and again; the line, sometimes reeled in, sometimes stripped in to keep the fish from getting slack, neither overran nor tangled. The little rod, staunch as a bull dog, took the strain superbly, ready to spring back to the perfect straightness which is one of its delights, and the tiny hook held on.

Five minutes passed. The fish was tiring. I could see him now. A frantic effort to get under the sunken log failed, by the narrowest margin. Now he was at the surface and near the bank. Now he saw the net, and in an instant was once more in the middle of the pool. Now he was back again, and in the net, and on the bank, and after the rim of the net had put him to sleep, in the creel, and under him and over him fragrant grasses all beaded with the rain.

He was no giant after all. A pound and a quarter— not more. But light tackle makes heavy fish, and I had all the fight and fun with him I should have had with a trout of twice his size on a four ounce rod. And that was not the end of it. Before I wended my wet way home, there were seven trout in the creel, a man in the little flivver happier by seventy times seven than when he set out, and another story added to the annals of the great little rod that Rubia gave me.

A Bum Story

YOU'D better go back and finish your nap," said
Captain Harry Smith, as the fishing launch Carnegie
nosed her way into the dock whereon the subscriber stood
in the cold gray dawn, and likewise in the wind and the
rain of a vicious northeaster.

"You finish your nap, and I'll take off the pulpit," said
Harry.

Which I did, and he did. And when both operations
were completed, the breeze of wind was still on the job,
and fishing had a visibility of just exactly zero.

Not a boat had gone out of the Old Harbor at Block
Island, and they all lay huddled together—the Two Friends,
the A-to-Z, the Hilda & Vanna, the Addie Mae, and all the
rest, and rocked and rolled behind their three breakwaters,
according to their custom when the weather is bad.

Which reminds me of another boat commonly known as
the L. A. Moore. The name on the stern is L'Amour. But
that is neither here nor there.

So Captain Harry started to take off not only his sword-
fishing pulpit, the swordfish season being over, but also his
bow-sprit, whose end it adorned, while I put on the re-
mainder of the clothes I had with me against the cold,
meandered over to the Island Department Store, and bought
for five cents a pad of yellow scratch paper, on which these
lucubrations are being set down.

I can see the Old Harbor from where I sit, with its sea-
wall made of the same brownstone they used to build man-
sions of on Fifth Avenue, and the ripples racing across its

[14]

I Never Was Fast to a Really Big Tuna

surface in the heavy gusts. An occasional fisherman in oilskins yellow as my paper moves deliberately about his shore concerns. But for the most of them it is a dies non.

The window behind me opens on the foam of a perilous sea, smashing, and spouting, and hissing against the rocky breakwater and the sandy shore, as the long rollers reach their appointed end.

The harbor scene and the sea are Simon-pure and honest-to-goodness, one as truly as the other. Even in a north-easter, this place suits me down to the ground. But what you miss in a gale is the smell.

Block Island is a little dab of gravel and boulders, sand and clay, dropped by a glacier in a careless moment fifteen or twenty miles off the spot where now the town of Newport lies with its yachts and its villas, and at least a million miles away from everything that Newport stands for in your eyes and mine. On Block Island live about a thousand thrifty New Englanders, who make a frugal living, some of them from their little stone-walled treeless farms, more of them from flocks of equally frugal summer boarders, but most of them from the eternal sea.

I like Block Island. I like the Block Islanders, and some of them seem to like me. If I didn't, I wouldn't have been going there every chance I got for the last twenty-five years. What do I go for? Bums.

Many long years ago, almost before the Horse Mackerel of old times had become the Tuna of today, I rowed ashore at the Old Harbor, alone in a little dory, just as the gray dawn was breaking. How and why is no part of this story. But from then on I caught the said Tuna in quantities on rod and reel, and was happy.

I in my simple ignorance supposed them to be first among game fish, and I cheerfully pumped them up out of the bottom of the deep blue sea, where they shook their heads and fought doggedly on even when their fight was about over.

Pumping, if you should happen not to know, consists of lifting your rod with all your strength and then reeling in hard as you lower it, thus with much labor retrieving a little line. Candor compels me to admit that I had a grand time doing it, and achieved much healthy exercise thereby. In the words of the old song, other love I did not know.

But one year when I couldn't get away any earlier, I came to Block Island in September and caught a fish that wasn't there at all in the summer months—a fish that made an epoch in my angling history.

Like the Tuna, he was of the Mackerel tribe, but as different from the Tuna as a rapier from a meat axe. The meat axe properly handled is a formidable opponent. So is the Tuna. The meat axe has sterling qualities, and commands respect. So has and does the Tuna. But no meat axe is really beautiful. And the Tuna is a stubby fish, almost as big around as he is long. There is nothing rapier-like about him.

Now I admit that comparing a Tuna to a meat axe isn't fair, and it isn't right. A Tuna just out of water is very good to look at, very good indeed. But I am trying to make a point, as others have done before me, and you must make allowance for that.

The Tuna has power, no end of it, and his stubbiness is relieved, as they say of yachts, by a fine exit. Considering how thick he is in the middle, the Tuna is not such a clumsy-looking fish. And he can fight—how he can fight! As a combatant, and also as a comestible, he is entitled to no mean consideration.

But isn't the Tuna the hardest fighter of all? Perhaps. Perhaps even the Broadbill Swordfish, which also belongs to the Mackerel tribe, may not be his equal pound for pound. Some one else must pass on that. I have fought a number of fights with Broadbills, but never was fast to a really big Tuna.

What I started to tell you about, however, wasn't Tuna, but great Tuna's little brother, whom I first met and fell for at Block Island many years ago. Not about the meat axe but the rapier.

Those were the days when light tackle meant nothing lighter to me than a nine-thread line, with a breaking strain of two pounds to the thread. I imagine it was on the nine-thread I first took this gateway to more fun than you can shake a stick at. And I imagine the weight was about twelve pounds, for that is fair average. At any rate it was an amazing experience. Nothing like this marine comet for speed, gameness, and beauty had ever met me on the rolling ocean before that memorable day.

At Block Island the name they give this swift-darting arrow among fishes, this compendium of all the qualities a sportsman most admires, is Bum. Bum! Just that.

And what is it they dishonor with such a name? A slim graceful glory of a fish, deep rich green on the mottled back, on the belly pure blinding white shot with rose, and with black spots like finger prints on either side, as though it had just escaped the grasp of an amorous Nereid.

The markings about the forward half of him look as if some good fairy had poured over his head the most beautiful stir-about of iridescent colors that Queen Mab herself could ever imagine, so as to make, as it were, a mother-of-pearl sundae. From the head the gorgeous mixture has dripped down along the sides, and you can see plainly where it ceased to run over the less brilliant surface beneath.

And if I wished to express to a Block Islander the fortunate fact that I had been so blessed as to attract and capture one of these masterpieces of the Almighty, I would say: "I caught a Bum."

Swift as a falcon, too. Such swiftness is no accident. This fish is stream-lined as no air-plane ever was. The back fin drops down into a groove which hides it altogether. The ventral and pectoral fins have depressions into which they fit, so that not the least obstacle to speed may interrupt the glass-smooth outline when speed is called for. Even the eyes are molded to exact conformity with the general surface, and the small mouth when closed, the gill covers, and all the rest sink and merge into the perfect figure of this living torpedo.

And this speed-fish has not only speed, but speed on the surface. This flying jewel fights his fight on top of the water. Where he strikes in his first slashing attack, just beneath the shimmer of the sea, there he will be when his war is over. You will never have to pump this fellow up from among the sculpins and lobsters twenty fathoms deep. He does not like such company. His place is in the sun.

Beauty and swiftness ought always go together, and here they make a faultless match. And all to the end of speed—speed and more speed, to the infinite delectation of the fortunate angler.

But who was this marvel, and what was his name? Not Bum, assuredly. Bum! what a name for such a fish as Homer might have sung—swifter than swift-footed Achilles, and more beautiful than Helen, whose beauty launched a thousand ships.

The Block Island name told me nothing. There was no better reason for this insulting epithet than this: the flesh is dark and over-rich, and brings little in the market.

I didn't know the right name, and what is more I couldn't find out. I searched the fish books, and once I thought I had it—Frigate Mackerel. There was a name to fit—free, swift, graceful, roaming the Seven Seas, as this fish does—Frigate Mackerel, of course. But I found out that a Frigate Mackerel is even smaller than a common mackerel salted in a kit. My mistake.

So when I caught another Bum—Heaven save the mark—I sent the best description of it I could make to the National Museum at Washington. No result. Next season I had my new find photographed and sent his picture. Still nothing. That left me with just one card to play. The season after I forwarded a specimen of the fish himself.

You know, or maybe you do not, that in the eye of the naturalist a specimen is a label with an object of natural history attached. What I really did was to send the object with the hope that Washington would supply the label. And this time the name came back.

It wasn't by any means a satisfactory name, and it didn't tell any story. But such as it was, it was the right name. Little Tunny. The Little part of it was right enough, because this wonder is no giant. But a tun is a big barrel, and Tunny sounds like a little barrel, fat and unexciting and slow, which is precisely what this fish is not. And the Latin name is still worse—Gymnosarda alleterata, which being translated is something like Letterback Naked Sardine—Naked Sardine because that's what Gymnosarda means, and Letterback because Alleterata is the Sicilian name of this world encircling phenomenon, and refers, I suppose, to the markings on the back, which you might take for writing if you had never been out of Sicily.

Letterback Naked Sardine! Thus do great scientists

abuse their power. At least that awful appellation isn't tatooed on, and in time even scientists may repent and bring forth works meet for repentance by choosing a name that fits. Here's hoping.

But after all there's mighty little in a name, as some one has suggested before me, if I'm not mistaken. The play's the thing, and the play in this particular case is simply superb. You must play a Little Tunny yourself to get the taste of it.

Unlike his close cousin the Tuna, this fish of my affection plays out his play, as I have said, at the surface. No pumping him up out of the bottom, which is the curse of Tuna fishing. And for the qualities that make a game fish, I challenge you to find his peer, in salt water or fresh.

Believe it or not, this wonder among fishes will take out in his first rush two hundred yards of line, sometimes two hundred and fifty, and one memorable run stripped three hundred and fifty yards of six-thread line from my spinning reel, as near as I could guess. And I didn't miss it much, I promise you.

That fish deserved to get away. He did get away, and I'm glad of it.

"But what's the use of talking? What do you say we go catch one ourselves, you and I?"

"All right, come on."

So off we went, and this is the story of the day.

It was just after Labor Day. Not a summer boarder, not a girl in shorts remained to dilute the Block Islandness of the Old Harbor. There was hardly a breath of wind. A little haze half hid the horizon. Outside the breakwater there was a swell, of course. There always is at sea. And you are out at sea the minute you leave the harbor at Block Island. But there wasn't a ripple on the surface.

A BUM STORY

I love those smooth glassy undulations, and the way they step up the colors they reflect from the sandy cliffs at the south end of the island. The fish bite better when there is a breeze, but in this life you can't have everything just the way you want it. Maybe you've heard that before.

Our lines were in the water as the Carnegie rounded the breakwater buoy. But what we looked for first wasn't fish, but birds. For where there are fishing birds, biting fish are apt to be not far behind. As we left the Old Harbor the only bird in evidence was a solitary Herring Gull, flapping its wings in a bored sort of way, and obviously not going anywhere in particular.

The land fell behind us as Captain Harry sent Ezra to the masthead. On such a day we might easily run across a Swordfish, and a 400 pound Swordfish amounts to something at forty cents a pound on the dock.

Pretty soon Ezra hailed the deck. "Shark!" called Ezra.

"What kind?" said Harry.

"Hammerhead," answered Ezra.

"No good," said Harry. "It won't bite."

So we let it alone, and passing close aboard, watched its stubby back fin and pointed tail, separated by four or five feet of water, gently cutting the surface, as the Hammerhead sculled its weaving way along in its unceasing journey through the sea. If it had been a Mackerel Shark, Harry would have got out the Shark bait he keeps all ready on a wire leader in a pail of ice, fastened it swiftly to a heavy rod, and dropped it overboard. And then you'd have had your work cut out for you.

A Mackerel Shark is a fighter more formidable than a tarpon, and almost as good a jumper. And if you had hooked one you would have remembered it till the cows came home. Likewise you would have remembered the

[21]

piece of it you would have had the luck to eat broiled for your supper. Mackerel Shark is practically as good as Swordfish, and I can't say more than that.

But the Block Island Hammerhead, as Harry said, won't bite, and I'll bet it's no good on the table. I never tried it.

The crisp air of the morning was getting warmer, and the sun climbed fast.

"You'd better put on your smoked glasses," said I. "The glare on this kind of a day is mighty hard on the eyes."

So you got them out and put them on—a troublesome job, with one hand conscientiously holding on to your rod all the time. Not a little tackle has been lost overboard when the angler wasn't tending to his knitting. Then for a while nothing happened.

Suddenly "Birds to the south'ard," came down from the masthead. Harry swung the tiller with his knee. Pretty soon we could see that birds were there, lots of them. There was going to be something doing.

"Better reel in," said I. "Perhaps there's a bit of seaweed on your hook. If there is you might as well be towing an empty line."

Away in the distance were excited birds, and under the birds, splashes. Here and there came a vivid flash, like a window at sunset, as the light rebounded from the smooth skin of a jumping fish.

"Bums," says Harry. And that put ozone in the atmosphere with a vengeance.

For all practical purposes a fish is as big as your tackle is light. The lighter the tackle the greater the skill, the longer the fight, and the better the sport. You can get just as much of a battle, and a far more interesting one, out of a twelve pound Little Tunny on a six-thread line than you can out of a fifty pound Tuna on a thirty-six.

While the birds and splashes are still afar off, let's have a look at the rod and reel I use for this supreme fighter. My rod conforms to the Tuna Club 3-6 specifications—not over six ounces in weight, and not less than six feet long, butt and all. Split bamboo it is, for a hickory rod of that weight and length would be too limber even for me, to whom stiff rods are an abomination.

My reel is a No. 6, a little over four inches in diameter. And it holds first a lot of old line for backing, and on top of that 500 yards of six-thread Ashaway linen line. With the backing, the six-thread just comfortably fills it up, allowing for the fact that wet line takes more room than dry. But the essential thing about my reel is that it has no handle drag, as most sea reels do.

When my reel gets into action, the handle spins backward or I wind it forward, as the case may be. It's a little harder to fish with, I admit. More than once the whirling handle has dusted my knuckles, and once I paid a finger nail for my infatuation.

Nevertheless I regard a handle drag as an invention of the devil, except for very large fish. It gives the fisherman an undue advantage, as I see it. But like other modern machinery, I suppose it's here to stay, at least till somebody invents something that will give the poor fish even less of a run for his money.

My reel is simple and straightforward; it keeps you in closer touch with the fish; and at the same time it gives your quarry a little better chance to get away. It's a sporting proposition, and for years I haven't used anything else for little Tunny.

Before the Carnegie was out of the harbor I'd doubled your line for you at the seaward end with a knot I learned at Catalina. After the five or six feet of doubled line comes a swivel, and after that four or five feet of fine steel wire, about as thick as the wire of these invisible hairpins that ladies affect. I am a married man, and I have a right to know.

At the tail of the wire is one of those Japanese white feather baits that are used so widely these last few years. Much as I hate to admit it, they're a long way ahead of the Pinchot lamp-wick bait, which had all other Tuna baits faded, if I do say it, till these Jap contraptions came along. The feather neither twists nor untwists your line as most baits do; and the lighter the line the easier it gets twisted.

But sometimes, when the Little Tunny are feeding on very small bait, they won't take even the feather. If that happens you are not beaten yet. Search your tackle box for a diminutive tin Mackerel jig, scrape it till it shines, and try that.

During the foregoing exposition the launch was running six or seven miles an hour—almost her best. But her best is just a saunter for Tuna and Little Tunny. Harry had a short hand-line out from the stern with a cedar jig. Your line and mine, with trolling drags set, were out on either side.

Yours was to starboard, which is easier for a right handed man, and it was longer than mine. I saw to that, because in my experience the line farthest back gets the most fish. Being a green hand, you were entitled to the edge. If you'd been an old hand, our lines would have been even, and you may lay to that.

By now we had got up close to where the voracious birds were slamming themselves down on the water and into the school of bait. And there were acres of Little Tunny— literally acres—breaking, and swirling, and throwing themselves out of the water in their fierce desire to kill.

This was no more a glassy sea. The great deep was broken up, or at least the top of it was. Just to look at it was excitement enough. The Little Tunny flashed and smashed here, there, and everywhere, as the Hags and the Herring Gulls from above plunged their heads under after the same bait the Tunny were gobbling from below, and then paddled frantically over the surface to launch themselves in the air for the next plunge. Here was life on the ocean wave and lots of it.

There wasn't another fishing boat anywhere near us, so Harry took his time. While you and I held our breaths and hungered for a strike, he skirted the school instead of running through it; and that's good judgment too. Running through a school will drive the fish down if you keep at it long enough, or if enough boats are doing it at the same time.

Nothing happened for an interminable half-minute. Then suddenly there was a huge swirl just behind your bait, and a flash of light as the striking Tunny showed his silver side. You felt a touch and nothing more. But your heart moved up into your throat just the same.

In another second came a yank, as if your hook had snagged a derelict, only ten times more vicious. This time there were no missed connections. The handle of your reel spun till it was nothing but a mist, while the line melted away like butter on a flapjack.

"Yeeow," I shouted, in the yell I always yell when a fish strikes.

"He's got it," said you, in a distinctly tremulous voice. "What'll I do now?"

"Throw off that trolling drag," hissed I in your ear, "and let your thumb just touch the line—only just. Just enough to keep the reel from overrunning." And I suppose I said it about six times on end. You needed all six.

Your line was fading, vanishing, disappearing till your whole being cried out to stop it.

"Clamp that thumb down hard," says the Natural Man. "He'll have your whole line in ten seconds more. Stop him quick."

"Well, you can try if you want to," says I over your shoulder, knowing from experience what was going on in your head, "but if you do, bang goes your line, and off goes your fish."

While you were wild to use Force, and I was talking Skill, your fish was taking line in a rush no other fish of anything like its size could begin to equal. A hundred yards, one hundred and fifty, two hundred, perhaps two hundred and fifty.

"My gosh! Gee whiz! Goodness gracious! Heavens to Betsy!" and other lady-like expletives burst from your quivering lips. I was behind you and I'll give you the benefit of the doubt. Something unusual seemed to be going on, and to you it seemed to go on for hours.

Would this demon fish never stop? Would the line never cease to fade? I know as well as you do how it stirs a man up inside. But when you could hardly bear it any longer, at last the reel-handle emerged from the mist. If the fever called running wasn't over for good and all, the temperature was distinctly lower. Perhaps you could even recover a little line.

Harry had stopped the engine the moment your fish struck, and the boat was lying still.

"Wind in if you can," said the Experienced Fisherman from somewhere behind you, "but wind in gingerly. Be ready to drop the handle and put back the thumb the minute your fish shows signs of starting off again. And if he wants line let him have it. Give him plenty, just so you keep in touch with him. You've got all day to bring this fish to gaff."

Your leather rod socket was belted over your right shoulder and under your left, and not around your waist. That brought it high on your chest, where the short butt of your 3-6 rod would meet it handily.

"Set the handle of your rod in the socket," said your Adviser in Ordinary, "and keep the point up. Gauge the pressure on your line by the curve of the rod. And when the fish jerks his head, or runs, or otherwise raises Cain, let him have line. You might have heard me say that before. Give him line when he wants it, till you begin to feel that you are master."

So you let him have line, but not because you really wanted to—far from it. Then suddenly your line went slack. At that your internal organs, with one accord, turned to mere water.

"There!" More Heavens to Betsys. "He's gone." Despair in every syllable.

"I don't think so. Reel in hard. You feel him again? Good! He's on yet. You can't expect him to swim the same way all day. Your line went slack when he changed his direction toward the boat."

That change helped you to win back perhaps a hundred yards of line. A hundred yards away your fish was flashing along just under the surface about as fast as ever, and your line, straight as a taut wire, was cutting the water till the spray rose in a little cloud behind it.

"You got line enough back on the reel that time so you can afford to be a little rougher. Give him thunder with discretion. Get in every yard you can. But Man, keep your rod up. And glue your eye to the bend of it. You're

[27]

not handling a derrick. Pretty soon the fish will turn, and the line will come easier."

Upon which comforting words, Whiz! He was gone again in another hundred yard rush. Your comment on that I refuse to recall beyond this: "What in Tophet am I going to do now?"—much the least reprehensible part of it. I'll concede now that you were in one difficult spot, but of course I wouldn't admit it at the time.

"Lift your thumb. Let him go. You can either let him run or lose him. It's up to you."

About this time your recovery from shock had proceeded far enough so that a man could understand snatches of what you were saying.

"Good Heavens! Isn't this fish ever going to give in? Durn his pictur'. Have I got to give up all this line I worked so hard to get? This blame fish must have a dynamo in his tail. I never felt anything like it. There he goes again!"

Zzzz! Zzzz! Zzzz! In one yard and out two was the way it seemed to you, which was a jingle I hadn't intended. Your rod was bowing like a headwaiter, and your line was streaming out to sea.

"The very devil must be in him." And then to me: "How long have I been at this thing? It seems like a week."

Well, you'd been at it just seven minutes, and the worst was yet to come. And so for minute after minute (of sixty minutes each) the fight went on, sometimes the fish on top, sometimes the fisherman. Fifteen minutes, twenty, twenty-five, and still the fish was going strong.

But at long last most of your line was back on the reel. The fish was near the boat. Everybody shouted at once, "There he is." We could see the glorious creature gleaming in the sunlight as he fought on his side in the final circling which all rod fishermen at sea learn to know so well. This was the last phase.

"Stand up," said I, "and fight the rest of this fight on your feet. You'll see why in a minute."

I'd hardly spoken when your fish swam right under the launch. What to do? What to do? Anxiety—no, consternation—covered your shining, not to say perspiring, countenance. You were earning your fish in the sweat of your brow for a fact.

"Plunge your rod into the water straight down to the reel," said the Embodiment of Wisdom, "until the tip of it carries the line below propeller and rudder, and below the splinters on the keel. And as the fish swings to the other side, follow round the stern without lifting your rod till the line is clear, and be ready to repeat. Which you couldn't have done sitting down.

"Right at the boat is where rods are broken and fish are lost. Don't press, and mind your P's and Q's."

To which excellent advice you answered nothing. You were very much otherwise occupied.

Circle followed circle, and then more circles. You thought you had him, over and over again, and said so. And each time you just barely didn't. It was tough, and on that point you did not keep your sentiments to yourself. The Naked Sardine wasn't the only one the strain was telling on.

Finally the knot of the doubled line appeared above the surface. Harry picked up the gaff, seized the line, worked down it till he could reach the swivel, leaned over the still struggling fish, struck in the gaff, and the fight was over.

Yet as the gaff lifted your hard won trophy into the boat, disaster missed you narrowly. You forgot to lift your rod at the same time (or perhaps I forgot to tell you), you forgot to let a yard or two of line slip from the reel, and so Harry's swing that brought the fish aboard bent and almost broke your tip. It wouldn't have been his fault if it had. And under any rules a broken rod disqualifies the fish.

But you had the luck of a beginner, and there was your prize, beating the planks with the very last of his fading strength. And the sigh you heaved of pure relief would have made a tidal wave if the tide had been running the right way.

All this time what had I been doing, besides telling you what not to do? Well, I had a strike the moment after you did, and hooked my fish, and to give you free play I'd just been keeping in gentle touch with him, letting the line fight him till the bell rang for the last round. I was having more fun watching your troubles than over my own affairs.

You hadn't noticed it, having something else on your mind, but my fish too had been circling about the boat, just like yours. More than once, when the circles crossed, I had to pass my tip over or under yours, or drop it deep in the sea, to keep the two lines from getting all snarled up.

Now that your fish was on deck, I was ready to bring in mine. It only took a minute or two, or maybe three, for the line had pretty well worn him out. And here they were, the two of them, as like as peas in a pod.

This was my time to clinch the argument.

"Are you ready to admit that Little Tunny is the gamest fish that swims?"

You hadn't caught even a reasonable percentage of all the other fish that swim, and I hadn't either. But even if you hadn't, I had you in a cleft stick. You were ready to swear that not in the Seventy-seven Seas was there a fish

This is the Bum that Beats Them All

to hold a candle to this one.

What else could you do with your hands still aching and your breath still coming fast? And anyway it was the truth. This is the Bum that beats them all.

We shook hands on that, and then it was time to get busy again. Into the well the two fish went. Harry straightened your wire, a little bent at the end of the fight. I straightened mine. In went the clutch, and we were off after the school again, which was still chasing the unfortunate bait under the insatiable cloud of birds.

It took you a full half hour to get your first fish, and no wonder. The next one came a little easier. Experience teaches. I have taken several in three minutes and a half, and one in three minutes. But for a while yet your average time would not be far from five times that.

The travelling disturbance in the ocean produced another and still other Little Tunnies, which came to gaff in due season. The sport seemed to be set for all day when in a moment, in the twinkling of an eye, the birds were gone. We didn't see them go. They just weren't there any more. All at once the world was empty. Not a fish broke the surface, and nothing troubled our baits.

Noon came. The march of the Carnegie through the polished pulsations of the sleeping ocean went steadily on. Not a bird. Not a fin.

Time for a meeting of the Society for the Dissemination of Useful Information.

"What I didn't try to tell you," said I, "when you were in the throes of battle, is that an educated thumb is the prime factor in light tackle fishing. The thumb does it. Myself I shave with an old-fashioned razor. Stropping it has made a callous on my right thumb that counts against me. There's the only argument I know of for Mr. Gillette's machine tool, that takes the romance out of shaving.

"In my assumed capacity," I went on, "as past pluperfect master of the game, which Heaven knows is pure assumption, I have already helpfully indicated to you that in light tackle fishing the main pressure on the fish comes from the long dragging line. The strain is greater the nearer the hook, and lightest at your hand. Usually it is all the pressure the line can stand, and often more.

"Now if perversely you add to the line's own drag the heavy brake of your thumb, your chance of landing a Little Tunny on light tackle will be about like your chance to land a whale. This is one game that has to be played according to the rules.

"Until he comes to think it over, every salt water fisherman is as greedy for line as any miser ever was for gold, and its just as foolish in one case as the other. The more line a fish is hauling behind him through the water, the harder the strain on him, the less the strain on you, and the shorter the fight. Watch that thumb. Let him have line. Cautious, prudent self-control is wisdom's root. Besides which it catches more fish."

To the foregoing diatribe you lent an ear with your usual politeness, but I could see there was a limit to your patience. Luckily for me, it came time to eat.

"What have they given you? You're staying at Ballard's? Then Lobster sandwiches, for a guess. If there are any better sandwiches produced on this mundane sphere, I never ran across them."

But before even one sandwich had passed into limbo, Ezra, who had been eating while you were fighting your last fish, yelled down from aloft:

"Bums!"

There wasn't a bird in sight; there wasn't a splash.

[32]

But on the agate surface of the unresting sea there was a long arrow-shaped ripple, hardly wider than a single fish at the point, but widening gradually backward to its limit of 75 or 100 yards. A solid mass of Bums, and on their way. These pelagic fishes are always going places.

"They won't bite when they're like that," said Harry. "But we'll try them anyhow."

And we trolled our feathers in front of them, and alongside of them, and through them with just exactly no result.

Thousands of greedy Little Tunnies, with thousands of empty little tummies, and not one will bite. Why? Heaven only knows. Perhaps they will when the tide changes. Perhaps they will if they strike into a school of bait. Perhaps a stray fish may take hold anyhow. Nobody can tell. It's just one of the million things about fish that nobody can tell.

"But," said I to you, although I knew you didn't think so, "we've had sport enough for one day anyhow. Six Little Tunnies in the well. And I'll bet a nickel, with no hole in it, that your hands and arms are good and tired, to say nothing of your back. You'll be stiff tomorrow, just as your nose'll be peeling, and your soul eager for more of this most delicate and delightful of all salt water fishing."

So ends this day. Amphitrite, chalk up one more Bum Fisherman on the slate behind old Neptune's door.

Chocoloskee

"THE catching of fish," said the Sage of Chocoloskee, "is but an incident in fishing." He told the frozen truth. To be out in the open where fish are; to watch them at their great business of living; to see them in the water or out of the water; to fish for them, and even to hook them and have them get away—all this is wonderfully worth while—wonderfully better worth while than merely to catch and keep the stiffening fading body of one of the most beautiful forms of life.

Unless, of course, you are hungry. That's strictly different.

At the Southern end of Florida, where the land is mostly water and the oysters grow on trees, there is a vacation ground so marvellous that the average fisherman you tell about it won't believe you. And no wonder. If I hadn't been there I wouldn't believe it myself.

For the most part this happy hunting and fishing ground consists of bays and tidal rivers, bordered by great stretches of mangroves. And it is as violently different from the rest of these United States as Death Valley from fields of waving corn.

The mangrove is the daddy of this region. The mangrove not only gives it its character, but its very existence. It is the cause of which this refuge of egrets is the effect. But for the mangrove, whose many-fingered roots reach out like hands to make new land out of the sea and hold it, the Southern end of Florida would consist of water, mud, and little else.

High on its innumerable legs, the mangrove drops its dart-like seeds into the muck beneath, where they stand upright, germinate, and make new mangroves to make new conquests from the waves. And in addition to making the land (or more accurately the swamp) in which it grows, the mangrove yields tanning material, fuel, mosquitoes, and coon oysters impartially and in great abundance. Tanning material from its bark; fuel from its wood; mosquitoes from the general environment it creates; and oysters in bunches often bigger than a man's head, hung from its arching stilts full in the airs of Heaven when the tide is low, and sunk in the sea when it is high.

The mangrove is a barrier not only to the sea, but to those men who do their business in shallow waters. For a human to walk through a mangrove swamp is almost impossible. A bear can do it, and in some way that is beyond my understanding, so can a deer. Birds can fly through it. But to any unfeathered beings with only two legs, the mangrove says, "You shall not pass."

Walkable land and drinkable water are the two great lacks and the two great needs of this remarkable Florida Gulf Coast. Chocoloskee Island has both. It lies in Chocoloskee Bay, a broad shallow sheet of water, distinguished from many another like it in Southern Florida by the fact that there is quite a lot of walkable land and drinkable water in its immediate neighborhood. On Chocoloskee Island there is a settlement of fishermen and a store. And Turner's River, the most wonderful tarpon ground I have ever fished, is there or thereabouts also.

One evening in early September, and in the long ago, we anchored near Chocoloskee Island in the houseboat KENNESAW—Anthony Dimock, Gilbert, Julian, W. E., and I, and the crew of the Captain's gig. Tarpon from

Turner's River was what Anthony had promised us. And tarpon from Turner's River is what he gave us in full measure, heaped up and running over.

But to catch tarpon was less an objective than an underlying necessity. We couldn't photograph tarpon unless we hooked them first, and what we needed most of all was tarpon pictures. A fish unphotographed left us cold.

So we turned in under our mosquito bars, made of cheese cloth because mangrove mosquitoes sail through ordinary bars without even the courtesy of a momentary hesitation, and let the disappointed myriads sing us to sleep. Few songs are sweeter than the song of the mosquito when you know he can't get at you.

Next morning we were off. We left the *KENNESAW* in two detachments—the cameraman with the other fishermen ahead, while I came behind with Tom Hand in Hugh Cooper's launch what the others were after was fighting and photographing some big fish we had seen in the river some days before, while I had fixated my libido on taking tarpon on a fly.

Fish are much wiser than you sometimes think. If you hook a tarpon and he tears up the surface of one of the narrow rivers of Southern Florida with the waves and splashes of his fierce efforts to escape, the other tarpon see or feel it. Anyhow they know all about it, of course. But what they decide to do about it is another matter.

They may be frightened or they may not. If they happen to be feeding at the time, they make fuss enough themselves to cover up the other fusses. The play of another tarpon on the line, the uproar as he falls back into the water from one of his tremendous leaps, his rushes on the surface or beneath it, all the mad commotion of his fight, disturb the feeding fish in no respect whatever. They also are doing their bit in the general upheaval.

But let the same hooked fish make the same disturbance in the same place outside of meal times, and there will be an instant migration of tarpon from that neighborhood— a migration which includes them all, from the largest and the wisest down to the most foolish youngster in the river. And if you keep on harassing them they'll stay away entirely. It is a common saying among the boatmen of Chocoloskee that the first day you get good fishing in Turner's River, the second day you get poor fishing, and the third day you don't get any fishing at all.

What Tom Hand and Hugh and I saw at the mouth of Turner's River after the other party had been disturbing the peace upstream for half an hour was just what I've been telling you about. Down with the falling tide came tarpon big and little, in droves and herds and hordes, driven out of their favorite feeding ground before the time. There seemed to be no end of them. Often as many as fifty were in sight at once as they rolled up to blow.

"Blow!" says you. "Fish have gills. What's this about blowing? What have they got to blow with?"

Hold on a minute. Tarpon have gills. That I admit. But tarpon have also rudimentary lungs, and that's what brings them up to blow, if they happen to feel like it. Sometimes they empty and fill those lunglets at short intervals, and often they rise to blow in little groups of five or six together. And since when they do the back fin and the tail fin look almost exactly alike, and since rolling fish are hard to count, when six come up you think you have seen at least a dozen.

Certainly there were plenty of them rolling on that wonderful day. But rolling tarpon, like barking dogs, seldom bite. In and about the groups of rolling fish I cast a silver-and-white bass fly with a brilliant red body, using a salmon leader and an 8-ounce Leonard fly rod. Not even the semblance of a bite did I get, although they seemed to have recovered entirely from their scare. So I changed my tactics, which is the mark of good generals generally.

Rolling to the contrary notwithstanding, a small piece of mullet told a very different story. Whole mullet was what the tarpon were feeding on, and when I submitted a piece of mullet as a sample they struck at it greedily. As the bait skittered across the water their lunges made disturbances like mine explosions, and not such little ones at that. They sent my heart into my mouth until I could just about taste it, even at the end of a trip filled with tarpon.

But to provoke a strike is only the preface to tarpon fishing with tackle intended for trout. You've got to establish connections with your fish, and with such tackle that's not so easy. At each lunge I would riposte with all my rod had in it, and the hook would fly back at my head minus the mullet and without a sign of tarpon attached.

The outside of a tarpon is iron-clad with heavy scales. The inside of him is just as heavily armor-plated—at least as far down as where he does his swallowing. That is one reason why any but baby tarpon are really outside the fly-rod class. With anything less than a heavy rod it is almost impossible to drive the hook home.

Finally one tarpon hooked himself. I was skittering my piece of mullet with a line little longer than the rod when a small fish rushed at it and missed. I kept the mullet going toward the boat. Once more the candidate for the ichthyic Valhalla struck and missed again. Then, with the rod and line straight up and down and the bait almost under the gunwale, this incontinent tarpon went at it again.

This time he got the bait. Also he got the rod. I ought to have known better. But I wasn't exactly what you might call cool. As it was, the fish yanked the perpendicular line and snapped the upright rod just below the upper ferrule. Then the broken piece slid down the line and frightened the fish into such frantic contortions that he promptly shook out the hook and was gone.

I was ashamed enough, but on the whole I wasn't sorry. I didn't deserve that particular tarpon. Anyway I'm all for giving the fish his chance. (That's the way to talk when you've foozled your chance.) There's ten times the sport in using tackle too light for the fish you're after, and ten times the satisfaction in getting him with it. (That's serious.) Telegraph poles may be all right for the man who can't catch fish with anything else, but me for the limber rod and the long fight.

So perhaps after all the rod was broken in a good cause. In spite of the disgrace to the fisherman who lets his rod get smashed (meaning me), I rather think the game was worth the candle, especially since, the break being near the ferrule, it was easy to serve the pieces together and go on with the day's fishing.

Turner's River taught me one thing at least: If your rod is a fly rod, point the tip of it at the bait and strike from the reel. For that's the only way you stand much chance of hooking a tarpon on light tackle. I tried it as soon as the break was mended, and shortly after landed a 3-foot fish. Score one for the eight ounce Leonard. Things were starting off well.

The next tarpon was a slender brilliant jumper, four feet and one inch in length, who actually came high out of the water as many as thirteen times. Not even a flea could beat that. The quarter of an hour it took to quiet this acrobat sufficiently to unhook him and turn him loose was good enough to make up for many broken rods.

Like nearly all the tarpon I have ever caught, this fellow lived to fight another day. Perhaps I'll find him grown a foot or two longer on some future visit to Turner's River. Or maybe you will.

About this time the other *KENNESAWS* came down the river with pictures in their cameras and a gorgeous six foot seven inch tarpon in the boat. They were headed for Chocoloskee to have him sent by the fish boat to Marco for mounting. He was Gilbert's fish and was sure worth it.

While they were gone Tom and Hugh and I worked up the river to the one cabin that stood on its shore, and hung around it to see whether a great squall that was gathering would pass or strike. When we saw that it couldn't miss us, we went up and sat on the little porch, watched the storm clouds pile up, and listened to the man who lived in that pitiful shack tell about his troubles.

His troubles were extreme poverty and old age—that most terrible pair. And they certainly had him in their grip.

His outlook on life was anything but rosy, small blame to him. The shack he existed in, so far as we could see, had neither a chair nor a bed. A couple of planks, nailed to a cleat on the wall at one end and resting on a wooden horse at the other, made a place to lie down on. There was also a plank table. Wooden boxes served to sit on. A broken soap kettle stood on the porch to make smudges in, but there wasn't a scrap of mosquito net in the place.

It seemed utterly incredible that any human being would stay in that awful hovel who could possibly get away from it. The man we found there said he followed fishing mainly, and stayed there just for a place to stay in. He had been in the Navy three years and seven months, had visited China and Japan, and was bitter against the men who had made him keep clean, stand straight, and carry out his orders.

Next he explained that all would be for the best in the best of all possible worlds if only the taxes were taken off liquor, and saloons could sell untroubled by any license fee (this was years before the Eighteenth Amendment had been adopted and repealed). Later we discovered that somewhere in or about the premises he made illicit whiskey. For a man in that business his mind and manner of life seemed fairly normal after all.

The storm, and a most gorgeous and satisfactory storm it was, assuredly did not miss us, and it was all the lunch we got. But no good fisherman would make moan over that.

As soon as the downpour was over we set out trolling from the launch. While I fished with the Leonard, Hugh Cooper used a Murphy split-bamboo light tackle rod, on which almost at once he hooked a tarpon that Tom Hand saluted as "Grandpaw". The name was right enough.

Before Grandpaw had made more than one feeble jump, Hugh handed me the rod. Landing tarpon on light tackle was not what he lived for. It was, however, exactly what I was there for, and I was more than glad of the chance.

Grandpaw exhibited merely a quiet and conservative preference for freedom. Three other jumps he made, but they also were unworthy of his tribe. Sedately back and forth he moved across the river, and for the forty-five minutes of his dignified resistance showed no further sign of violence than an occasional lifting of his head to blow.

The only trouble we had was in gaffing him, for the

water was deep maroon brown from the stain of the man-grove roots, and the fish almost invisible a foot below the surface. But Grandpaw came to gaff in the end, and I didn't turn him loose. He was six feet seven inches long, thirty seven inches in girth, and weighed one hundred and forty-one pounds, fourteen pounds more than Gilbert's tarpon, and had been taken on a light rod, which the other had not. I hadn't hooked him, I couldn't count him, but I hoped to have him mounted just the same.

While we were enticing Grandpaw to join us, a great school of mullet had come into the river. Now when a school of mullet meets a school of tarpon, the subsequent proceedings are calculated to engage the whole attention of all concerned. Business is likely to be better than good.

It is the nature of the mullet to seek safety near the surface. The curious jaw of the tarpon, opening almost in the top of his head, was doubtless developed with that fact in view. Thus the tarpon below, the mullet above, makes an ideal arrangement from the tarpon's point of view. The testimony of the mullet has not yet been entered on the record.

The scene for the coming tragedy was marvelously set. Above the waiting river, untroubled by drop of rain or breath of wind, hung heavy clouds left by the storm. Beneath the dark sky lay the ominous black water, polished as glass. Around were the gloomy mangroves, shutting in the view. Not a leaf stirred.

Into this tense quiet of stream and air and forest burst the wild struggle for existence of eater and eatee. In a flash the calm was broken, smashed, gone. Life and death had turned themselves loose.

The river, so still an instant before, now was furrowed everywhere with long swift-moving zig-zag ridges of shining water, made by the unseen mullet darting with incredible swiftness just barely below the oil-smooth surface. At each instant and each angle of the flight a great boiling from below showed where an avid tarpon had struck and missed—or hadn't missed. Beneath the dark mirror of the river, fierce pursuer and desperate pursued filled the whole atmosphere with the drama of capture and escape.

Here and there, a dozen at a time, the mullet, hopeless of safety below, flashed above the surface in long low curves, twenty feet from start to finish, in their literal leaps for life. Here and there only did the tarpon show themselves, but the whole river was alive with the evidence of their power.

This outburst of tremendous vital action in a shallow stream, scarcely a hundred yards across, was impressive beyond telling. The play was vastly greater than the stage. It went on for hours, we thought, but in fact for tens of minutes only. We could not fish while it was on the boards.

I shall never forget it, and doubtless I shall never meet its like again. Not one among the five or six of our party with decades of experience in Florida waters had even seen its match.

It was a good day, a great day—good to the last drop. After the mullet had been scattered or eaten up, the tarpon were once more willing to consider bait, and two other Grandpaws took a fancy to mine. The first of them answered the sting of the hook with a leap at least eight feet clear of the water. It was magnificent, no less. But he was off the hook on the second jump, leaving the mental picture of that great leap behind him. But on such tackle that's what you expect.

Then a small fish struck, was hooked, jumped, and

escaped and we all were glad to see him go. What we wanted was big game on tackle designed for smaller fish, and the big game did not make us wait.

Again another Grandpaw took my mullet, felt the steel point, and made a splendid low leap across the surface, but half a man's height out of water—a vivid demonstration of power such as even the highest jump can seldom give. How long it was I cannot tell. That was no time to deal in feet and inches.

Again the fly rod failed. And by this time you must be convinced that what I was trying to do was not catch tarpon, but merely exercise them on tackle far below their just desert. And can you say it wasn't well worth while?

With the lunging leap of the biggest of the grandpaws the long day ended. The tide had changed, and most of the fish had gone out of the river. Soon after our time to follow them arrived. And as we went in the falling dusk the white herons under the dark mangroves shone almost like torches along the route of our triumphal return.

Catching fish, as Anthony Dimock said, is indeed but an incident in fishing. What I remember best in that wonderful day on Turner's River is not the fish we conquered and released nor the many little and the two big tarpon that struck, fought, leaped, and got away. It is not even the great fish I caught and kept. However deeply they left me in their debt, they were not the climax of the day.

What I remember, far beyond the fascination of the angle, is the marvelous intimate glimpse of wild life, as the tarpon and the mullet lived it and died it—wild life in action, furiously busy with its own concerns, with survival and extinction, with capture and escape, and wholly unaware of the human looker on. It is also the majestic oncoming of the great storm, the untellable colors of the sleeping river, the intimate contact with things outside my own concerns, and the sense of close participation in an alien world.

Moreover, after we left the *KENNESAW*, all that day I saw not even one mosquito. To the man who knows his Florida that means a lot.

Pelican Bay

THE National Forest Commission was looking over the Government timberlands of the West in the Year of Grace 1896, and I will say for it that it kept moving. At the time I write of we were concerned with the southern part of the Cascade Forest Reserve in Oregon.

One of the other members had been delayed, and those of us who had gone ahead were waiting for him at Pelican Bay. His delay amounted to a special dispensation of Providence, for it gave me altogether the best half-day's trout fishing I ever had.

Pelican Bay has been sold and bought since then, and doubtless by now is a different place altogether. I am writing about it as I knew it forty years ago, for I haven't been back since. It opens into Klamath Lake, which is a great body of water growing into land. The streams which fall into it are wonderfully clear, yet they carry fine silt enough gradually to change the Lake into a marsh, which in the process of time will change again to terra firma.

At the upper end of Klamath Lake there are already vast meadows, miles in extent; and enormous stretches of bulrush (tule, in the local phrase) show where the next meadows will appear. Some miles to the north are the great Klamath Marshes, which prophesy a gloomy future for all the water in the lake.

The lake itself, with an average depth of ten feet, is an incomparable breeding ground for trout. These Klamath trout are reported to reach a weight of fifteen, twenty, or even thirty pounds, and in their shape and color, and in the quality of their flesh, they are more like salmon than any other trout I ever saw.

Pelican Bay has many little arms, and at the head of one of them a great spring sends a strong gush of water, three or four feet in diameter, straight to the surface through the clear depths that surround it. When I first saw it, it was full of trout swaying about in the rushing current till I had to look more than once to make sure they were not living fish. In fact they were not live trout, but strings of silver cadavers, huge fish consigned by the men who caught them to the cool water as to an ice chest. And more beautiful fish there could hardly be. It was a sight to startle any angler to the deepest depths of his enthusiasm and it certainly stirred up mine.

About the spring someone had built a shanty or two, and provided a chance to eat and a chance to fish. To this little settlement came Oregonians on vacation (you can call them Webfeet if you want to take the risk) with their families, to spend a week or two in the open air. They camped socially together on a little plot of ground, fished from daylight to dark, and with their blessings were perfectly content.

Nowhere in America, except on the Pacific Coast, was it then the common custom for whole families to move into the woods for weeks or months at a time to rest and grow strong in the open air of summer or fall. Thank Heaven that good habit has at last come East.

In spite of their alleged webbed feet the campers needed boats, and there were boats near the spring. After dinner I made sure of one of them. My friend Will Steele volunteered to do the pulling. He said he didn't want to fish. Then at the little shop where repairs of every kind were tentatively attempted, I had a dented ferrule of my much-travelled rod made straight. After that I was ready.

It was a good rod, and it had cost me all of four dollars. It weighed $4\frac{1}{2}$ ounces, was built of lancewood, and was as limber as a politician's conscience. My confidence in it had been growing through the course of the summer, but I confess that I joined in the general attitude of scornful amusement with which the onlookers regarded the proposed attack of such a weapon on the giant trout of Pelican Bay.

The said onlookers did their fishing with codfish lines. A trout no sooner struck than he was hauled into the boat, or torn loose from the hook, by main strength and awkwardness. The advantage of this sort of thing over catching real codfish-balls codfish lay wholly in the surroundings, and by no means in the fishing. If you like that sort of thing, why, that's the sort of thing you like.

Steele and I followed the little arm down into Pelican Bay. The marvelously clear water showed us trout, few and small at first. Of course I had to try for them. But the sun was shining, and they merely ran away from my fly. There was nothing strange in that.

Farther along larger fish began to scurry over the bottom. In the Bay itself great schools of them swam by, big ones from two to ten pounds in weight, they looked to me; and here and there a monster that seemed even larger. They had their own business to look after, and it had nothing to do with flies.

But matters of interest under the water were not the only ones. An old Klamath squaw paddled past in a dug-out, with a fat papoose contentedly chewing a white tule root in the bow. She was coming for the fish heads the white man wouldn't eat. Dead heads are easier to collect than live fish. One more way to live without work.

Ducks in multitudes were making a deafening clamor. But ducks I'd seen before. What I never had seen was flocks of stately white pelicans dozing on the glassy water, or spreading their huge wings and rising slowly far ahead of the boat, till they sailed motionless into the hazy distance. That was something to write home about.

In the air the pelicans seemed enormous, like tent flies in a hurricane. I never imagined any bird could look as big.

Not even their size, however, was half so exciting as their organized fishing. These flying table cloths were like the hornets in the story, and like the hornets they got results. And this was how I saw them do it, and more than once:

Six or eight pelicans would form a line beginning in very shallow water and extending out at right angles to the shore. Every bird was headed the same way, and every bird moved steadily along, keeping in perfect alignment with the others. It was like the drill of a squad out of a crack regiment.

What was it all about? Fish. It was a fish drive, pure and simple. And if one pelican didn't get a fish that met that line (that is, if it was small enough so he could swallow it), another did.

I couldn't see the fish, but I could and did see pelican after pelican plunge his beak in the water and then lift it to high heaven. And if that didn't mean swallowing, what did it mean? The trout those pelicans must have destroyed would be enough to drive a fish commissioner to drink.

Pelicans must know a lot, and here was the proof of it.

But while I watched the pelicans, I gave my fly no holiday. I whipped the water earnestly and in many places, but nowhere could I get a rise. At last it was plain I must choose between trolling and no trout. The trolling had it.

In my fly-book was a little spoon. I put it on. For some time nothing happened. Then Bang! a vigorous strike. After that nothing happened some more. My limber rod had failed to hook the fish. It had that one bad habit.

But better luck was on the way. A second tug! I struck in answer. A fish like a fresh run salmon threw himself two or three feet into the air, shaking his head savagely. Again and again he broke, wasting his strength, until there was little of it left, and I could steer him gently within reach of the gaff after not more than ten minutes of a fight. The little rod was doing magnificently, for that trout weighed eight pounds!

Nothing like that had ever happened to me before. I was in the seventh heaven. Like the lady whose boy friend ordered a plate of ice cream with two spoons, I was glad I came. This was the sort of fishing I had dreamed about.

Strike after strike followed in quick succession. The sun was going down and that explained it. I struck and struck until the limber lancewood hooked a second trout. It was a lively scrap while it lasted, although No. 2 weighed less than half of No. 1. But a trout of three and a half pounds on a four and a half ounce rod is not to be sneezed at. And I was a very long way from not sneezing at this one.

No. 2 landed, almost at once a third trout was hooked. He didn't break and I saw only the flash of his tail as he went down after the strike. But I could feel that this was serious.

From the beginning this trout's strategy was better than good. His first fierce rush came straight toward the boat, and I should certainly have lost him if Will Steele hadn't pulled like a Trojan to help me keep the fish from getting slack line. He didn't, and the fight was still ahead.

After that first run, a few moments of inaction. The little rod was so far below the level of this fish that at first he refused to tire himself against it. Then came another fierce rush, but off to one side. The reel screamed, and the rod bent in nearly a complete circle as I gave him the butt. I had to. By no means all the line in the world was on my reel.

It was a straining minute, and more were on the way. Rush followed rush, and then more rushes, till it seemed certain I must lose him. There were no end of rushes up his sleeve. It was no trouble at all for that tireless fish to take out line, but lots of trouble for me to get it back.

Like the fighting in a championship battle, there was something doing every second. First the fish went after me, then I got back at him. But at the end of every round he seemed to be as strong as ever.

I wasn't—not by a jug full. My hands and arms were aching, and every minute seemed like a week. The fight went on interminably. And during the whole of this long-drawn eternity the fish resolutely refused to show himself. I began to wonder what on earth it was I had got hold of.

But this was no time for speculation. We were near the mouth of the bay where it was over a mile wide. The wind came up, and it took little time to kick up such a sea as we were obliged to take bow on. My unseen fish seemed to know all about it, for no sooner did it happen than he made runs to one side and the other and almost forced us broadside to the swells. If he had, we would have had to swim for it. My rod was too light to check him, my line was an H, the lightest size of fly line, and where he chose to go we had to follow.

Meantime heavy clouds had covered up the sunset, and the night began to fall. Heavy sea, heavy fish, and heavy darkness. It all amounted to a considerable set of circumstances. And all this time I hadn't even seen the fighter that was making all this fuss.

Only just before black night came down did he show himself. Compared to what he had been doing, at that first sight he looked small. His performance would have done honor to a ten-foot shark. Or that's the way I felt about it.

As the eternities drifted by he gained line but I gained more, until at length I had him almost at the boat. Not yet, however, within gaffing distance. At intervals his silvery side flashed in the little light there was as he surged to the top, and we could spot him for an instant. Except for that, the only indication we had was the bend of the rod, and the rod was almost invisible.

So was his back invisible, even when close to the boat, and the gaffer, with the fish within reach of his hand, couldn't see to strike. And I did yearn and hope and hunger to have him strike. You know how it is. You lift to the very limit of your tackle, and the instant you let up, down goes the fish again, as if he weighed a ton. And the next time you lift and let up, he weighs half a ton more.

This was the time for all good men to come to the help of the party of the second part, and Will Steele didn't fail. The wind fell a little, the sea grew less, and finally, what between good luck and good management, the gaff struck home and brought that gallant gladiator in.

The moment he touched the bottom of the boat Will and I almost fell upon him to make absolutely sure he didn't flop out again. And when we knew we had him for good and all, both of us broke into vociferous and discordant whoops in celebration of the victory. We couldn't dance, for the boat was too small and the bay was too rough, but we could yell—and yell we did, like a whistle on a tugboat.

When that part of the celebration was over, a combination of match and watch showed us that the fight had lasted one hour and forty-seven minutes. Whew! I dream of it yet.

We shook hands on it, and rested, and let the satisfaction sink in. There wasn't anything else I wanted in the whole round world. My cup was full. That's why I've told the story of that fight a thousand times, although more often to myself than to any listener.

How much did the fish weigh?

By George, I did forget to tell you. Nine pounds and a half, and I always thought those scales were wrong.

Two's Company

IT MAY be foolish to confess it, but I like to fish alone. Not, of course, if I can persuade Rubia to go along, and not always when I can't. For there are few things more delightful than to fish the right water with the right companion, whether on ocean, lake, or stream.

But for me there is a powerful charm in being solitary in the companionship of woods and waters or the sea. It may be the sign of a crabbed nature, it may be the mark of a soured disposition, it may be just natural cussedness, but at least I tell the truth about it. To know the woods especially, you must be alone in them, and you will never know them fully until you are alone in them at night.

Whether you approve or not, let it be admitted that I love to fish alone. Now fishing alone on foot, or even on horseback (which isn't as foolish as it sounds), is simple and practical from every point of view. But fishing from a boat is different. Moreover, pond fishing from a sturdy flat-bottomed skiff on a still day is one thing, while fishing from a light canoe in a breeze of wind is very much another.

A canoe is the most temperamental of all the craft that float. If it knows you and likes you, well. It will do anything for you, go anywhere with you, and ride out a sea that looks like sudden death. It will refuse to upset under the most aggravated provocation, will let you climb in again out of deep water if for any reason that might seem desirable, and will open to you more waterways to happiness than all the yachts of all the millionaires.

Here's the Upset the Camera Demanded

There seem to be no limits to the sweetness of a really kind canoe. I have seen Rubia take sharks of over seven feet with rod and reel from a canoe, and at the finish shoot them with one hand the while she managed the rod with the other. Meanwhile I knelt in the other end, like Patience on a monument, and kept my paddle in the water and my tongue between my teeth. But the canoe loved her, and sat up on the water like a church on a hill.

I have fought many a tarpon from a canoe, and landed not a few of them standing on my feet in it, rod in the left hand and tarpon in the right, up to ninety pounds in weight. The canoe liked me, and I never was thrown out till a movie camera came along and insisted on an upset. Whereupon the canoe yielded, and the overturn was duly photographed. You can see it, tarpon and all, in the picture.

The best harpooning I have ever known has been from a canoe. A porpoise at one end of the line and a canoe at the other will keep your mind off all your troubles. But why multiply instances? A canoe that really likes you in spite of all your faults is close second to a perfect wife.

But there's nothing more sensitive than a canoe, and never let yourself forget it. Any evidence of ill temper on your part it will instantly recognize and resent. Never speak harshly to your canoe, lest the next minute find you swimming. Address it urbanely and with deliberation, and it will eat out of your hand. Rub it, as it were, gently between the ears, scratch it beneath the chin, keep your weight in the middle, and it will purr through the water like a kitten under a stove.

But the canoe with a hostile disposition, or even the canoe that feels a little strange—from all such deliver us. If you can not sell it or give it away, then take your courage in both hands and use an axe. There is nothing in this world more prejudiced than a prejudiced canoe, or that holds a grudge longer. If it does not get you today, it will tomorrow. Therefore beware. As the ancient Romans used to say: Cave canoem.

At Beaver Run there is a sixteen-foot canoe that gladly calls me Master when Rubia is not by. It is docile and considerate to a fault, and lets me walk about in it, and refrains from dumping me out when I drive it full speed against a hidden snag, or when I pole or paddle standing on the gunwales for a better view. It is more patient than Griselda and kinder than the most sugary heroine in all the works of Louisa M. Alcott or Mrs. Aphra Behn, on whom be peace.

The praises of such a character who shall celebrate, who shall fittingly recite? The lion of Androcles was not more devoted, the daughter of what's his name more filial. It is, as the reader has doubtless remarked before this, a perfectly good canoe, and why make all this fuss about it?

Into this canvas-covered paragon, when the time and the mood woo me to be alone, I put a long spruce pole shod with iron, a paddle (more as a precaution than because I mean to use it), a five-foot casting rod, the fly rod Rubia picked out for me, a landing net adapted to the monster pickerel I never get, and in a creel nearly all the plugs and spoons and fly-rod wigglers and other barbed atrocities I ever owned.

Into it also I put a coat, remembering that pickerel bite better toward evening, when it will be cool. I put it in the bow because it will be drier there, or else I put it in the stern because it will be drier there. Full well I know it will get wet enough in either place before I put it on.

Then stepping in with a show of careless ease, in case

there should be anybody looking, I fasten to the thwart near either end some eighteen inches of strong line tied to the neck of a little bag of gravel (shot would have been better). Then I am off.

When I have reached the spot where I propose to take the first pickerel, my pole goes deep down into the mud, and one of the little bags is given a twist about it. When it falls back into the canoe, I am at anchor, and there I stay, let the breezes blow how they will, till I have fished what water I can reach and choose to move again.

Just beyond where I am anchored the bottom slopes deeply into the old channel, which here is all of thirty yards across. This is the place to try a wiggler. So the casting rod flips it as far as I can manage, and I reel it in as soon as the back-lash is straightened out. For I have the faculty of getting more backlashes in less casts with more kinds of guaranteed anti-backlash reels than any man who reads this sad confession. I am letter-perfect at it. Yet I do sometimes catch fish.

Once, just hereabout, I was casting with a wiggler ring-straked and speckled, when there came a check, not solid as when you hook a stump, but yielding and alive. The line began to cut through the water, but without the proverbial hiss. Speaking of which reminds me to say that I am skeptical of hisses.

You will recall perhaps that when Ajax hurled the great rock in Homer's Iliad, it was reported to hiss through the air, that Podbipienta heaved another rock in Sienkiewitcz's "Fire and Sword," that Iliad of the Poles, which also was made to hiss. Few self-respecting writers ever catch a fish on paper without a hissing of the line.

Myself, I feel like hissing all these hisses out of court. Even poetic license has no license to hiss. We have all heard a line sigh, and occasionally when a big fish has made a sudden dash right near the boat your line or mine has hissed, but mighty seldom.

All this time my pickerel has been surging against the rod. Now I have him almost within reach. As his smooth round back shows for a moment, I know him to be big. How big I'll never tell you. I'm all jazzed up about him. But the rod and the line are too much for any pickerel in weedless water, and he gains no single inch. Then into the net and into the canoe and on to the scales. His size is my secret.

I wonder is there anywhere a fresh water fish whose protective coloration is more perfect than a pickerel's? If so, it must be a frequenter of very shallow water, like the flounder, or the countless little fishes that disappear against a sandy or a rocky bottom. When the sun is shining squarely on the water in the middle of the day, you may see a pickerel where he lies, but not always even then. As the shadows lengthen, how many times have you and I had a strike close alongside the boat, and have seen nothing more than the complete or partial disappearance of the bait, as the invisible jaws closed over it.

See that rotting stump of an old white pine. There ought to be a pickerel somewhere round it. I cast my wiggler so that it falls ten feet beyond, and drag it slowly past. Nothing? Then try the other side. Sometimes it takes a lot of teasing before you can make him strike. Or that's a likely opening among the lily pads. There ought to be a big one hiding there. Perhaps I get him, and then again perhaps I don't. And so when that place is fished out, the bag of gravel is unwound, up comes my pole, and the canoe takes me serenely onward to another spot.

Maybe there's something doing under that old log. Off

Three of Rubia's Sharks - from - a - Canoe

goes the wiggler on its predatory mission, and bang it comes down on top of the log, and, what's worse, a hook goes into a seam the weather opened. And I've got to go and lift it out. And if there were forty pickerel under the log I'll get not even a smell of them until the next time.

And so, with this and that, before the fish stop biting I have perhaps six or eight pickerel, perhaps but two. But few or many, I have had what T. R. used to call "a corking time". I always hate to quit.

A canoe and one is company, and no amount of pickerel can make it a crowd.

There is nothing better than such solitary fishing, except of course when Rubia comes along. One evening when she did, we took between us sixteen pickerel, enough for my brother's household and my own. Not one of them quite reached two pounds, and most of them were under one. We had more fun than if we had caught a hundred pounds of fish, twice over, and the whole world was filled with calm contentment as we paddled homeward in the twilight, bringing the captives of our rod and our reel with us.

Another time, as I sat motionless and alone, with not a ripple on the surface and not a living thing in sight, came the sharp whistle of a buck across the water. I never saw him, but he brought back memories that made the ants crawl up and down my back. Suddenly the familiar pond grew strange, the wood about it full of questions. It was like old days in the wilderness again.

Another breathless evening as a blue jay cried his autumn challenge in the thicket, a winged seed from a milkweed pod floated with slow dignity over the listening pond, and came unhasting to its light rest upon the silent water. Scarcely had it done so when over the hillside resounded the hammer stroke of the greatest of woodpeckers, and in a moment the Cock of the Woods flew wavily across and struck a new anvil on the other bank.

Then from the quiet distance three grebes came winging close to the darkening surface, lighted upon it without a sound, and on it drew smooth lengthening broad-arrows as they went about their noiseless personal affairs. A little breeze breathed and ceased. To move seemed like a sacrilege.

Such things are best remembered when a man goes fishing. As these and many another incident of quiet evenings serenely moved and lingered in my musing memory, while the light faded into darkness and all the world was still, a smashing strike in the lily pads brought me with a jar back to the earth again. Swiftly the rod bent to my hand, then to the fish, and the last pickerel of the day came in out of the wet.

By that time the pond had faded into unreality. Strangeness covered it as with a mantle. There was just light enough to puzzle the wayfarer on the long pole back, to shift the channel from where I knew it so well to be, and move all the snags away from their remembered lairs to new ambushes for the hurrying canoe, which still held fast to its angelic disposition, and kept me right side up and dry in spite of every trap. Right glad I was of that, and grateful too, for it was thirty miles to supper from the landing, and the nights were getting noticeably cold.

Of such times and places are quietness and peace.

Sea Bat and Whale Iron

EXCEPT for whales, walruses, krakens, sea serpents, and giant squids, which are not really fish at all, there are not many fishes in the sea whose weight is reckoned in tons.

As we came into Darwin Bay on Tower Island the very morning we first sighted land in the Galapagos, one of the ton-weights met us just inside the entrance. It was a sea bat or Manta or devil fish, or sea devil, devil ray, or pretty much any other name that suits your fancy. Obviously the men who named it knew little about it, except that (to quote Walt Whitman via Elmer Davis) it was something pernicious and dread.

This much named and much dreaded fish, which is said to destroy pearl fishermen by enveloping them in its vast wings (which I very gravely doubt), is a kind of exaggerated skate. Whatever else may or may not be true about it, its bigness and strength will not be denied by anyone who has had to do with it.

Darwin Bay is the crater of an old volcano, once full of fire, but now full of water. And full of sea bats too.

It is an eerie place. Around nearly its whole circumference are black basalt cliffs, too steep to climb, which fall vertically into the black water. What deeps lie below its surface we do not know, for the Naval officers who undertook to survey it found no bottom in the middle with a sounding line of 450 feet. What anchorage exists is very dangerous, with depths entirely misrepresented by the chart.

One edge of the vast crater is broken down into a passage that lets in the sea. Outside of its headlands on either side the great Pacific roll breaks over formidable reefs and against sheer cliffs and rock-piled points. Hidden behind bird-whitened rocks in an inner corner is the only landing beach, and there is nothing green about the shores but a bunch or two of Mangroves drawing a precarious living from rocks that seem wholly unable to support them.

In these surroundings, with a stiff trade-wind breeze blowing into the harbor, my son Giff and I went off that same afternoon to try conclusions, if we could, with a Manta, of which a new species had been reported from Tower Island but never taken.

We went with three others in a 22-foot Seabright dory with a 20 horsepower engine, which had been equipped for just such fishing, and we started to make the circle of the bay. The Seabright carried a tub of 200 fathoms of 12-thread Manila line, made to the specification of standard size whale line, and a whale harpoon and lance.

As I took my place in the bow of the launch, with a coil of line in my left hand and the hickory harpoon handle laid across the gunwales, it all seemed too good to be true. After long years of planning and waiting, I was in the Galapagos at last! And almost in the bodily presence of the great sea bat I had dreamed about so often and with such great desire.

And it kept getting better and better. Within a very few minutes we caught sight of one of these huge incredible fishes, whose fin tips were breaking water every moment as it waved its wings in a motion that looks just like flying. It seemed simply enormous.

Also it seemed fearfully strange—pernicious and dread, and no mistake—a creature from the antediluvian world

Manta by the Ton

that somehow had survived into our time. A thrill crept up my spine. This was what we came for.

Soon we could see the outline of the great fish through the dark water, as it swam slowly along. It was like a barn door just under the surface—a big barn door—or, more exactly, like a slightly warped square with only three corners, the fourth cut off to make room for the cavernous mouth with its two arm-like, fin-like feeders, and at the opposite point the long slim tail serrated with prickly spines.

The Manta paid us no slightest attention. I imagine there are few things it ever has to dodge. It was so fearless that I have no doubt we could have driven the launch squarely over it.

I saw that everything was clear, the line running freely through a heavy iron staple in the bow, the line knife ready to cut if necessary. I braced myself, raised the harpoon in both hands, balanced it, pointed with it at the fish to guide the steersman, and waited. But not long enough. As the event proved, I was too much in haste, and made the mistake of throwing too soon.

My left hand guided the iron, my right, its palm against the butt of the harpoon pole, drove it with all the power I had. It seemed to strike just where I aimed, and checked and stood and quivered for a moment before the Manta snatched it under water.

But somehow, I could not tell just how, the throw must have gone wrong. The fish was fast, sure enough. In a powerful, driving, surging rush it took out 200 yards of line in spite of the best we could do to stop it. The launch began to move briskly through the water behind the flying bat. We settled down grimly to the long task of landing our game. And then the iron drew.

All we had to show was the shaft of the whale iron bent

into half a circle. Whatever the reason, our fish was gone. Hard luck, however it happened. But the fisherman who cannot take hard luck with the good had better not go fishing.

We dropped no tears—indeed, we had no time. For the line was hardly coiled back in the tub and the soft iron shaft straightened before another Manta hove in sight. Again the examination of our gear, the tense approach, with Giff in a silent fever of excitement, and the driving throw.

Again the iron seemed to go right home. Again the fish was off in its tremendous rush, which actually reeked of power. Again we settled down—and again the iron came away.

It seemed as if the devil was in the fish as well as in the name. This was getting decidedly monotonous.

I have often noticed that bad luck runs out if you keep going long enough. Far off in the middle of the bay still one more sea bat showed its black wings. Here was one more chance, and this time something serious had to be done about it.

Everything was ready once more. We started for the game full speed ahead, and in our zeal we almost overran it. Suddenly, deep in the water, I caught a glimpse of its great back melting out of sight across our bow.

There was no time to take aim, and barely time to throw. But this time my luck held good. The pole stopped short with a sort of chug, as well-thrown harpoons do—stopped as if it had struck bottom instead of the fish—and the line literally hissed through the chocks as the startled Manta tore away.

We tried to check it, but we might as well have tried to check an elephant in full career. This sea bat went as fast as the traditional land bat out of Hades. It went so fast than when it came to the surface for an instant to thrash about we could hardly believe it was ours, it seemed so very far away. Then it was off again.

Gradually the fish changed its course, but not its speed, until it was headed straight for the reef at the northwestern headland of the bay, over which a very vicious surf was breaking. Already the water was decidedly rough and rapidly getting rougher. It began to look as if we would have to choose between losing the Manta and losing the launch, in which case we should have lost the Manta also. The prospect left something to be desired.

If, however, the harpoon had a solid hold, there was still a way out. We shifted the line rapidly to the stern of the launch and headed her, first under a slow bell, and then at half speed, as straight away from the entrance to the harbor and the sea bat's apparent destination as the pull on the harpoon line would let us steer.

At first it was nip and tuck, with the odds on the Manta. Then the engine began to prevail. First we stopped the fish from dragging us into the breakers. Then we began to drag it away from them. But only a very little at a time. Then the strain on the line grew so severe that we were forced to slacken, and the Manta started again for the open sea. Then we stopped it and started it back. It was pull monk, pull devil, for what seemed the long end of eternity.

But gasoline and machinery in judicious combination were stronger than even the great sea bat. Time after time it came to the surface thrashing violently, then yielded to the steady pull of the engine, never ceasing to swim away from us and constantly lifting the long points of its wings in violent protest above the broken surface of the bay.

Without the engine we would have had no chance at all. But with it, by and large and on the whole, we gradually gained line, slowly brought the Manta under better control, although it kept its strength amazingly.

We saw the reason when it appeared that the harpoon had almost missed it and was buried not more than a foot or so inside the after margin of its right wing and not far from the tail. It had no wound that could affect its vitality in the very least, and we simply had to work it down by main strength and awkwardness.

Even after an hour and a half the tension on the harpoon line was still tremendous. Although made to hold a pull of 1,500 pounds, it was close to its limit. Under the strain that part of it which ran from the boat to the fish had grown noticeably smaller than the part still in the boat, and it began to look as if the line might break or the iron might pull out.

So at Giff's suggestion we sank a second iron in the fish, this time a Block Island Swordfish dart, and fastened our possible and prospective prize to the launch with a second line. And it was more than lucky that we did, for only a few moments later the whale line parted, and only the line to the dart remained. Without it we should have had nothing left of our fish except the story of how it got away.

At last with some difficulty we worked our way through the reefs of the northwest corner of the bay toward the landing place. A few moments more, and we had the Manta in the cove and near the beach. The launch nosed up on the sand. Three or four of us swung ashore through the light surf, collected reinforcements from the party already on land, and six or eight men finally succeeded in landing the prize, this time really ours, far enough up the beach to be half dry between the swells.

Our Manta looked dead and acted dead. So we made

A Mouth Like a Suit Case.

sure that it was dead by bleeding it in the gills with the lance, for firearms we had none. A broad band of reddened water, with half a dozen sharks in it, floated off a hundred yards along the shore while we photographed and measured and marveled. It was by far the largest fish I had ever been concerned in catching.

Then I began to feel remorse, as in such circumstances I very often do. It may be no worse to kill a Manta than a muskrat—perhaps not half as bad. But I was not a little oppressed by the size of the thing I had killed.

The breadth across the wings was fifteen feet, seven and a half inches. It was just fifteen feet from the end of one of the feeder fins near its mouth to the end of its tail. Its thickness through was over two feet.

As it lay on the white sand the thing looked simply prodigious. Its color was a very dark grey or black, the pigment carried in a thin slimy outer skin that came off easily on our fingers. It was covered all over the back and the top of its wings, and partly also under the bottom of the wings, with very fine prickles, which cut our hands, as we tried to turn the fish over, until they were almost as rough as the skin itself. Its enormous mouth, about the size and shape of an ordinary suitcase, was roughly two feet wide, with the eyes set in line with it just at the outside base of the feeders.

The two feeders or lip fins, rolled up, looked like solid horns five or six inches through, but unrolled they became two wide flippers, most convenient, if that is what they happen to be used for, to shovel food into the cavernous mouth, which had no teeth that I could see. I have since learned that the Manta's teeth are small, flat, and tubercular, which last implies no reflection on the general health of the fish.

[67]

We cut out the harpoon and planted it in the head to have something to pull against while we tried to drag the Sea Bat out of water, but eight men could scarcely budge it even when half afloat.

Then, having photographed its back, we came to the question of its species. Every other Manta I had ever seen was black on top and white beneath, but this one, at least so far as the wing tips were concerned, seemed to be black on both sides.

It was necessary to decide the question. So we hooked the launch to the Manta once more, shoved and pulled all together till we got it off the sand, towed it out into deep water, turned it over (which eight or ten of us had vainly tried to do ashore), and beached it again, belly up, and photographed the curious pattern in white which occupied the center of the under surface. All the rest was black.

In the two stomachs, for it certainly seemed to have two, there was nothing but an oozy mass the color of puree of carrots and of just the same consistency. From the strong smell I judged it was composed entirely of macerated shrimps. We saved a double handful of it for the information of the National Museum, for not much is known about the feeding habits of these fish.

The last thing we did with the Manta was to pull it out into deep water, where I hope the sharks got it before it could drift back to poison the beach. But even if they did not, the birds would take care of it, for the grey Galapagos gulls were already at work cleaning up what small pieces the dissection had left lying about while the great fish was still ashore.

Raie au beurre noir (skate wings with brown butter) is a favorite dish at bourgeois restaurants in France. So that night we had sea bat wing for supper. I have tasted worse and also better. It was streaked like bacon and rather tough, by no means delicate in flavor, but perfectly sweet and edible nevertheless. On the whole I prefer shad.

Pictures of both sides of this fish, measurements, a large square of skin showing the white markings underneath, a generous helping of the puree of carrots, and the long tail with its curious boss near the root have all gone to the National Museum for study. What they found we shall know when their report comes in.

In the meantime I allow myself to cherish the fond but most probably delusive hope that the first time I ever took a Sea Bat may have served to introduce a new species to the scientific world. But whether or no, it certainly was a good fight.

There are plenty of Mantas in the Galapagos. We saw them not only at Tower but also at Seymour and Indefatigable, at Charles and on both sides of Albemarle. We could easily have taken more of them than we did, for I think we have learned how.

Ever since harpooning Mantas became the favorite sport of South Carolina planters in the spacious days before the War, down to the time when Theodore Roosevelt harpooned one himself while he was President, and up to the present day, no one to my knowledge has undertaken to acquire a Manta with hook and line. But to take a Manta on a handline with a shark hook and a whole Grouper for bait would seem to be a reasonable ambition for any man who likes his fish in large consignments. It is one of the things I have listed for trial on my next trip to the Galapagos.

A ton or two of Manta on the end of a thousand feet of small sized whale line might be expected to furnish contrast to brook trout on a fly. But when I gloat over it on those fishing grounds of the mind, where most of us do most of our fishing, and picture myself to me drawing this particular Leviathan with an hook, that compote of shrimps in the recesses of the Darwin Bay Manta rises continually to haunt me. What if Mantas eat no Groupers? Even with the most laudable ambition to inspire you, you cannot bait a shark hook with a shrimp.

Fifty Years Ago

WHEN I was young I loved to skate where no skate tracks were, as every normal youngster should. I loved to travel the winter woods where no footsteps marked the snow ahead of me, and I love it still— I mean, of course, untrodden snow except for the tracks of those wild creatures whose sign tells a fading story of brief moments in their lives, or of the manner of their death.

I have always loved to catch fish where no fish are supposed to be. To take out of a place too shallow or too public or too little promising to be fished by others, a fish good fishermen have passed by, still warms the cockles of my heart, and has through all my fishing life.

One summer fifty years ago the Pinchot family was slowly perishing of malnutrition at a hotel in Keene Valley in the Adirondacks. Economy amounted to a vice in that most frugal hostelry. The hostess, Mrs. Smith (to give her that unusual name), when one of her gaunt flock asked her for a match, would grudgingly unlatch the gate which led behind the counter, open a drawer concealed behind it, extract a single match, come forth with smiles bearing her precious gift, and bestow her bounty on the anxious petitioner. Lavishness could no further go.

Just across from this safe-deposit for matches, and close to the main road, there lay a rough and lumpy bit of meadow. Through it, so deeply cut into the soil that the casual wayfarer was unware of it, meandered a little brook, here choked with grass, there opening into quiet pools—

but always serene and clear. From the long perspective of today I think of it as very lovely. Then I had other views about it.

Poking about, as a human boy should do, I found this brook. I was, as I remember it, hunting for turtles, always a favorite game of mine. But turtles there were none. What I did see, as I peered over a hummock, was a trout, perhaps seven or eight inches long (a trout may easily grow an inch or two in fifty years), that slid into sight and out again while I watched him.

You know as well as I the mixed feelings of such a moment. Prickly excitement, fear of scaring the fish, haste to get tackle and come back and catch him, and the anxious exhilaration that such a find would normally provoke in any boy who loved to fish. I can remember backing carefully and successfully out of sight—and then I sprinted.

Where I found rod and line is beyond my recollection. But there emerge from the mists of antiquity the pursuit and capture of a grasshopper, the careful impaling of him on the hook, the anxious approach, and the dropping of the bait upon the pool. I take credit for having done it without raising my head high enough to see anything whatever of the brook.

But what I couldn't see, I certainly could feel. The trout was just as eager as the boy. He bit, I jerked, and the result was wholly satisfactory to me, whatever the trout may have thought about it.

After an interval of oblivion, I remember returning to the hotel in a state of great pride and exuberance, bringing my captive with me and being congratulated and made much of by a family which did its duty with a generosity that should provide an unforgettable example. Next to food, and by no means far behind it, praise is what the young most ardently desire.

And speaking of food, the trout was cooked, the trout was eaten, and the saving Mrs. Smith undoubtedly was spared the expenditure of provender to the value of several matches. Which should have won me her approval also.

It may have been this incident that led my Father to give me, a few days later, my first fly rod, and to take me with him into camp on the Upper Ausable Pond. Being what he was, however, I think he would have done it anyhow.

The road from Keene Valley to the Lower Ausable Pond has loomed in rocky grandeur all my life as the roughest road I ever traveled. My Father and I walked over it rather than sit in the bucking buckboard, and so did Judge William Hammersley of Hartford, the third member of our party.

The Judge was no lightweight in mind or body. I remember my astonishment when one of our two guides, who had spent much of his life with a traveling circus, picked up the Judge's 250 pounds or so and carried him across a stony brook with the greatest of ease. I never knew whether the flying trapeze, which my old nurse used to sing about, had anything to do with making him so strong.

I remember also the swift and sensitive Adirondack guide boats, the lean-to on the shore of the Upper Pond, the deep and delicious balsam beds (which I still know how to make), the camp fire and the flapjacks (the first I had ever eaten), and the huge square cake of maple sugar which supplied our syrup, with many a broken fragment for me besides.

The wilderness had not vanished in those days. There were still panthers in the Adirondacks. One night we heard a panther scream. What a thrill! The impression it made upon me was as lasting as a footstep in wet cement. It will remain till my very substance is worn away.

Another night we heard what the guides said was the call of a bear. Whether they were right, I do not know. At any rate I have never heard its like again.

These calls of the wild came from the steep dark mountain slope across the lake, in full view of our camp by day. At night stories of hunting and fishing passed the time about the fire till the booming of the bullfrogs sent me to bed.

In the morning and at noon, in the cool clear water, the chubs, gathered and waiting for scraps at the very brink, provoked in me a furious interest. They would even run in and out between my fingers in search of food. I could feel them and even catch one now and then if I tried.

Another matter has not escaped my recollection, and for good reason too: Innumerable black flies, midges, and mosquitoes worked their wicked will upon us. They were like a cloud by day and needles of fire by night, and they bit Judge Hammersley's hands until they swelled up like puff-balls—and finally tormented him into a fever. They took their toll of me likewise, and that's even a better reason why I've not forgotten.

Flies or no flies, that trip gave me a new and lasting conception of the wilderness, and not improbably it had much to do with making me a forester.

It was at the big pool at the inlet of Upper Ausable Pond that I took my first trout with a fly. There began a career as a fisher with feathers that has not yet closed.

The rod my Father gave me had a hickory butt, a second joint of ash, and a lancewood tip. What became of the other joints, I'll never tell you. But the butt reposes, ferrule gone, in my rod rack, and, like the old horse turned out to grass, in its senectitude has naught to do but enjoy its well-earned rest.

What I most wanted was a one-pound trout. I made a fetish of a one-pound trout. I think I saw a one-pound trout under the alders of the inlet far above the pond. But no such giant fell to my rod on that expedition, and the trip was plenty good enough without it.

One day as I sat casting in the big pool at the inlet, my Father was talking with Judge Hammersley in another boat a long bow shot away. Suddenly I heard him say, "The boy doesn't fish as if he were only thirteen."

My Father never knew I heard him, but the still water carried the sound, as still waters do, and gave me something to stiffen my backbone then and now and all the years between. It is a very pleasant memory.

The moral of all this is not hard to read: Whenever you go, and whenever you can, take the youngster along.

Under the Birds

WHAT do those birds say?" I asked Amaru as our twin-engined launch speeded after a flock of sea fowl of various kinds that was obviously following a swiftly traveling school of fish.

"They say tuna," said Amaru. "May be we ketch up, may be not."

And not it was. The tuna were traveling faster than we were and the best the launch could do wasn't good enough. So away went the tuna and the birds with them, and we were left with nothing to look at but one of the most gorgeous scenes in all the world.

To starboard lay the island of Tahiti, a green jewel set in a silver sea, its mountains lifted into the clouds, its groves of coconut palms lining the shore and bathing their feet in the quiet waters of the lagoon. Against the reef which bounded it the great white horses of the enormous swell flung out their manes, and the off-shore wind tossed them in a misty curtain thirty or forty feet in air.

Between us and the reef, the swells now hid, now lifted into sight half a dozen diminutive canoes, one man in each. They were fishing in the Tuna Hole, that deep depression in the sea where, as the natives believe, the tuna go to sleep. With a handline many fathoms long, a man may get a bite from a tuna awake enough to smell the bait, and be well paid for his trouble if he lands a single fish in a day.

To port, ten miles across the glassy but unquiet sea, lay Moorea, whose mountains, almost always hidden in clouds, today offered the whole of their impossibly fantastic outline for our contemplation and delight. Moorea, with its sharp-toothed peaks and overhanging cliffs, is like an extravagant backdrop for the wildest melodrama. It is one of the things that must be seen to be believed.

In such a scene, on such a sea, Charles Nordhoff and I, with Amaru and a couple of boys who went along whether we needed them or not, were looking for bonito or whatever we could find.

We were after the fish whose forebears had thronged these seas for uncounted generations. And with us were men whose ancestors for uncounted generations had gone after bonito and tuna and marlin by methods and with ceremonies which had taken milleniums to develop, and which, until the white man came, seemed likely to remain unchanged for milleniums to come.

Fishing in the South Seas was not merely an occupation. It was an art and a mystery. Nordhoff makes that plain in his discussion of *The Off-Shore Fishing of the Society Islands*. Bonito fishing in particular has been developed to a degree that is no less than amazing. It goes far beyond the complications of the most recondite and refined fly fishing of today.

Consider, for example, the bonito hook. A bonito hook is a narrow curving piece of pearl shell about three inches long, cut through the thick portion of the shell and running toward the thin edge, with a hole for the line at the thick end, and a barbless point sticking up from the concave side. It is a superb bait—not quite a spoon, not quite a jig, but not so unlike either.

There are scores of different varieties of pearl shells from different islands and different grounds. Each variety yields bonito hooks in four or five shades of color. And each hook is given two names—one personal to its owner —a nickname, so to speak—and one belonging to its peculiar shade and origin.

A particularly good hook becomes famous, and is handed down from father to son. Nordhoff speaks of an Hawaiian legend to the effect that one old chief, a mighty fisherman, had a hook of such attraction that the fish leaped after it into his canoe.

Says Nordhoff: "Eight years of fishing with the natives have convinced me that the fish recognize instantly the correct shell for the conditions of weather, time of day, and the small fry on which they are feeding. * * * Often out of a dozen hooks available aboard a canoe, there will be only one at which the fish will strike freely; yet all twelve have been chosen by an expert fisherman."

"* * * Sometimes when only an occasional bonito will strike, the expert hastily opens the fish he has caught in search of roe. If roe is found he compares its color with his hooks until he finds one of precisely the same shade. Such a bit of shell, it is thought, will be seized without hesitation."

Every slip of shell carries its barbless hook, usually of iron or copper, the sharpness and the angle of which with the shaft must be exactly right. The hook should fall from the fish's mouth while the hooked bonito is being swung aboard, but not so soon that it will fall into the water.

In spite of modern wire, the old bone point still holds its own today. I have one made of a pig's tooth. At one time they were often cut from human bones, and were highly prized. Men with dark skin and curly hair were believed to furnish the best bones, and the story is that the bones of ancestors were sometimes used. When a friend asked for the loan of such an ancestral hook, the point was taken off and all he got was the shank.

The rods are chosen with great care from the best specimens of a special grade of bamboo. The reason is that the splinters of a broken bamboo are razor-sharp, and may cause painful damage.

Commonly the rods are from fourteen to sixteen feet long, or longer for a man of unusual strength. The line, a foot shorter than the rod, is made from the fibrous inner bark of shoots of ro'a maohi, rolled on the maker's naked thigh, and almost always three-ply. As with hooks and rods, in the old days an exceptionally good line was given a name, but now rods and lines are nameless.

Three, four, or even five lines are attached to each rod, the points of the hooks caught in holes at the butt while not in use, and the pearl shanks carefully covered with hibiscus leaves to protect their delicate shadings from over-exposure to the sun.

In old times the opening of the bonito season was a religious rite. On the first day just one boat's crew went out. All the rest of the island remained ashore in complete inactivity and silence, and the entire catch was offered in the temple. Next day the same observance was repeated, but the catch was given to the chief. The third day the season was open to everybody.

Luck was not wholly the fisherman's affair. Failure to play the game on the part of his women folks while he was away was believed to bring bad luck or even disaster. If a bonito was hooked in the lower jaw, which seldom happened, it was a sign that things were going wrong at home. And this belief is fully alive today.

The man also has his responsibility. If he quarrels with his wife before putting to sea, he'll catch no fish. Pity the feminists have been unable to transplant so wholesome a belief. And if an enemy spits on a canoe as it lies hauled up on the beach, that canoe's luck is seriously impaired.

You know about Charles Nordhoff, from whom most of the above bonito lore is taken, or you ought to. He is the man who, with James Norman Hall, wrote *Mutiny on the Bounty* and *Men Against the Sea,* which latter is by far the finest story of life and death on the ocean that ever came my way. Also those two are responsible for much good reading besides. They work together in the most successful collaboration I know of—but they play apart.

Jimmy goes to the mountains, Nordie to the sea. I'm for the sea, like Nordie. And that's how he and I happened to be fishing for bonito together.

Meantime our launch had covered many miles of empty ocean. Then someone shouted from the bow. Eyes more keen than mine had seen more birds. Soon even I could pick them up, and Amaru began to tell us what they had to say to him. And what the birds said was this, "Bonitos, but no bites".

Anyway we took a chance. Amaru opened the throttle, we caught up with the school, we did our prettiest, but nothing happened. The birds had told the truth.

How the birds said it, and how Amaru read it, I know only in general. Such exact interpretation of fish and bird psychology and behavior is beyond me. It has to do with the kinds of birds, the way they fly, their height above the water, and the degree of excitement they show. What was Greek to me was clear to Amaru, Tane, and other native fishermen.

Over and over again these men told me by the birds what fish were in a school, and whether they would bite or not, and did it long before they could see the fish at all. And they never missed it once.

This amazing ability to read the birds was developed from sheer necessity. Before the white man came, and for generations afterward, the canoes in which the Tahitians fished for bonitos had to be paddled at high speed, sometimes for hours, before they could catch up with a feeding school of fish. But if, when the school was reached, it was made up of tuna too big to handle, or of bonitos that wouldn't bite, that prodigious labor was in vain. Failure to understand the language of the birds brought a high penalty. And so they learned to read it.

The school of fish that Nordie and I were following went down without contributing the least excitement, the birds scattered, and once more the sea was void.

But not for long. In the far distance another flock of birds appeared, told Amaru there was sport ahead, and communicated its eagerness to our whole ship's company. The twin screws roared, and Amaru prepared for serious business. In came my feather bait. My modern tackle was laid aside. This was to be Tahitian fishing.

Amaru began to finger the heavy bamboo rods whose lines were not native fibre, as they used to be, but heavy cotton codfish line. Each bamboo was equipped with several lines and several of the barbless nacre baits I have already described. The lines were just a bit shorter than the rods. When not in use the point of each hook was caught in the butt, so that each line dried under tension and never kinked when the war was on.

A piece of canvas, stained and weather-worn, was thrown over the cockpit, seats and floor. I thought it was to keep them clean of slime, but blood was what Amaru was mainly thinking of.

By now we could see the spreading splashes as the bonitos drove after the bait. Above them the frantic birds were streaming in close bands over the water, and diving into it, and hurling themselves upon it in little groups so dense there was hardly room for them to open their wings. Where the fish were thickest the birds were thickest also. They were too wild to pay us the least attention.

One bunch of forty or fifty were so furiously occupied that they hung on until, from where I stood in the stern, they disappeared under the bow as the launch drove straight at them. We must have missed them by the skin of their teeth.

Now we were in the school! The time was past to think of birds. Bonito were all about us. Amaru stood at one rail, I at the other. We trolled our baits in zig-zag lines behind us, fully as ardent as the birds.

A bonito swirled at Amaru and missed. Instantly another took his bait. With a mighty effort he snatched the eight pound fish out of the water and swung it struggling into the boat. It struck Nordie full in the chest, spattered him with blood from top to toe, and fell to the canvas. The barbless hook came loose and hit the water again before the fish had finished decorating Nordie.

Another struck at Amaru. Then one at me. I yanked. Out came my jig and nothing else. I snapped it back into the water. Instantly another swirled. He got my hook! I put in all I had, lifted him out and half-way to the boat, but he fell just short of it.

No time to weep. In a split second I had another. So did Amaru. My heave threw mine between our feet. That made three bonitos hammering the deck and throwing blood all over us.

It was the fastest and most furious fishing I ever saw.

Amaru, who had caught bonito a thousand times, was just as wild about it as the new chum from Pennsylvania.

In went my bait again. A bonito hit it like a thunderbolt, but before I could lift him a shark had bonito, hook, and all! Where the bonitos are the sharks are never far away. That's where the second line came in. In went its hook, and the wild sport went on without a pause.

While we were at it we saw another boat hurrying to reach our school—we saw it, that is, when both were on top of a wave at the same time—a launch with natives as thick all over it as sparrows on a roof. And every one of them wore a solar topee, a pith helmet, for no reason I could understand, and every one of them was full as good a fisherman as Amaru, or maybe better. And the way they welcomed those little fishes in was a caution to cats. We couldn't hold a candle to them.

Suddenly the school went down and left me breathless. Not another bite. Amaru had six bonito, and I two. And not so bad for a beginner, either.

Once more the sea was vacant. The great swells swept by without a ripple to break their metallic smoothness, except when a vagrant breeze fretted their summits with an evanescent ripple, and then smilingly died away.

It was a marvelous day, and the company was just as good as the day. I would have been happy with no fish within a thousand miles.

But fish were a whole lot nearer than that. Almost before we knew it more birds appeared and wig-wagged more good news, more splashes came in sight, more tenseness as the bamboo rods got into action, more strikes, more heaves, and more bonitos in the boat. It was the kind of fishing a man might give a finger for and not feel overcharged.

In the middle of that school were two great sharks, swimming around and around each other, obviously coquetting, and less occupied with bonitos or with us than with each other. I was hungry to strike an iron into one of them, but there was no harpoon aboard. We were organized for a different sport.

Among the bonitos of that school were tuna also. A big one (not for a tuna, but among bonitos) swirled at Amaru's pearl shell, and missed it. I would have loved to see him try to lift a 40-pounder aboard.

Then something heavier than I was looking for hit me. I put my back into it, but the best I had just barely lifted it aboard. It was a tuna of no more than a dozen pounds. Before I got it out of water, I would have set its weight at fourteen stone.

The native bonito fishermen use only one hand, the right, and the very best of them (Nordie says only one or two are left) used to catch each fish under the left arm as they swung it aboard. They say a good man could keep two fish in the air all the time, but you'll need help to believe that, and so do I.

I hadn't kept two fish in the air, or even one, but I had caught a tuna, and I was glad of that too. I was glad of it because I proposed to eat him raw. Which sounds as raw as the fish, but hold your horses. This is what you do:

Or better, watch Ai Yu, our Chinese cook. First he breaks up the tuna fish into little flakes, such as a boiled codfish separates into, and soaks the flakes for three hours in the juice of fresh limes. Then he cracks a fresh ripe coconut in two and scrapes out the meat of it with a special tool you'll find in every South Sea household. After that he squeezes the scrapings in a cloth.

Out of the cloth drips a white milky fluid, not colorless like the milk of a drinking coconut, but bluish-white. It is slightly tart in flavor, and one of the most delicious of all sauces. Ai Yu pours off the lime juice and pours on the milk. And then it's your turn.

What you can't eat of that ambrosial dish, I will. Not all the chefs of all the Kings of France could beat it. Fresh tuna (it must be fresh out of the sea) prepared as Ai Yu prepared it (cooked, if you like, for that's the effect of it) was altogether the best thing Rubia and I tasted in the islands of the sea. I got enough of it only when I could hold no more. And we never had it often enough to suit me.

Tuna is best for raw fish á la lime and coconut, but bonito runs it a close second. Humans, however, are not the only ones who like bonitos raw. Sharks regard them as highly desirable, and so do the great marlin that hang around the tuna and bonito schools and collect their taxes. What I wanted most was one of these monsters.

So we hooked a bonito on my heavy tackle, and repressing Amaru's passion for bonitos, still totally unslaked and ready to break out on the slightest provocation, we trolled conscientiously around and about every school we found, dragging the silver bonito behind us.

No good. No use. Nothing. Either there were no marlin there or this was not their day to bite.

But there are marlin in these waters, and no mistake. I saw one brought in to the dock at Papeete that weighed either 460 or 640 pounds. Take your choice—I can't remember which. And Zane Grey's world's record of 1,040 pounds, after the sharks had lunched off it, is the fish that made Tahiti famous. But how many months it cost him in time and how many thousands in dollars, I leave the

Great Exaggerator to relate.

But here's a fish story I think you may accept, although it strained my own throat a lot when I first tried to swallow it.

At Atuona in the Marquesas, before we reached Tahiti on our trip of 1935, Rubia and I ran across Monsieur LeBronnec, who, when we met him five years before on another island of the group, was working as a collector for the Bishop Museum at Honolulu. LeBronnec and I got to talking fish, of course, and he told me what follows:

A year or so before, a whaleboat, manned by natives, was fishing with a handline for a great marlin that was known to hang around the strait between Hiva Oa and Taku Ata. At nine in the morning they got a bite and hooked a fish. It was the very one they wanted. It gave them a tremendous fight that lasted all that morning and until half past one in the afternoon.

You must imagine all the details, the great surges of the giant fish, the straining struggle to hold him, how the line grew thinner and thinner under his power as hours went by, and the wonder that line and hook held on. LeBronnec never told me, for he wasn't there to see. But finally they brought the monster to the boat, lanced him, made him fast, and towed him into harbor. Then they hauled him out and measured him against the boat, now in its shed on the beach. The fish was two feet longer than the whaleboat, and the whaleboat was 36 feet long. Some fish, what?

LeBronnec said he had not measured the fish himself, a joy of which he would never have deprived himself if he had been like some fish liars I might name, and neither had he seen it before it was cut up, although he was living in Atuona at the time. But he had seen the enormous head, and he reported that a hogshead of meat—a hogshead, not a barrel—had been salted after this huge marlin had furnished forth a feast for a hundred people.

Another man who happened to come up while we were talking confirmed LeBronnec's story. It seemed to be well known and generally accepted around Atuona. But not by me. A marlin thirty-eight feet long? Three times as long as the biggest one I ever caught? That took some tall believing. And yet LeBronnec was obviously telling what he believed to be the truth.

But when I repeated this fairy tale to Eastham Guild, who has fished these waters for many years, and to Carrie Guild, who holds the world's record for women with a black marlin of over 800 pounds, neither of them batted an eye. They both regarded it as entirely possible. And Nordie, whose knowledge of fishing in the South Seas is unique, accepted it without the smallest hesitation. You can take it or leave it as you choose.

There is some evidence to back it up. Captain Laurie Mitchell, that supreme and supremely modest fisherman, hooked a marlin in Tahitian waters which was seen by him and several others. It was too heavy to jump, but it shouldered out of water enough to form the basis for an estimate. They set its weight at not less than 2,500 pounds. How close they came will never be known, for the great fish got away.

Some of these huge marlin, like some great sharks de par le monde (Port Royal Tom, for example), have a local habitation and a name. One of them is seen from time to time off the pass at Tautira on the island of Tahiti. Chief Rai Arii, who caught his first fish with rod and reel out of our launch and made a good job of it, knew all about him. And so did Nordic, of course.

Captain Cook anchored off Tautira, and lost an anchor there. It still lies buried amid the coral.

It was off Tautira that Rubia landed her largest tuna—82½ pounds. And the devil of it is this: her fish is six pounds bigger than my best. That tuna made a gallant fight, but not more gallant than she did. She handled the limber quick-taper rod like a veteran, and showed the tuna who was master. He wasn't among the big fish that got away.

Rubia beat me at Tuna fishing on this trip as she has done before. With her it's got to be a habit. I almost won the blue ribbon, but here's the gloomy tale of how I didn't.

Trolling one day in and about schools of bonito with Trader Baum (named by Carrie Guild for Trader Horn for no reason in the wide, wide world), I hooked a tuna and played him hard on the very limber rod which is my greatest contribution to sea angling. It was the same rod Rubia beat me with, and it gives you twice the power over big fish and twice the fun with little ones. But all that is beside the point and by the way.

I wanted that tuna as a kiddie wants an ice cream cone, and I played him hard. In thirteen minutes I brought him to the boat. And then, of course, I had to lose him. After the gaffer had the doubled line, the fish ran under the boat, caught the heavy 12 foot wire leader in the screw and snapped it and was gone.

It was my own fault I lost him. The gaffer was green, and I failed to tell him all about everything, as I am in the habit of doing when the gaffer knows all about everything already. What's more, I never even saw my fish— the sun-glare hid him—but the Trader did, and set his length at five and one-half feet.

[88]

That's no sardine. Suppose we lay the extra six inches to friendship and enthusiasm. The five foot tuna that remains is no chicken and distinctly visible to the naked eye. In any case this one weighed far more than I could afford to lose.

Well, all this time my bonito has been whirling behind the launch unconsidered and unscathed by marlin or tuna, the day has been passing, and it is time to start for home. But there will be no time when it's time for me to forget bonito fishing between Tahiti and Moorea, where the great glassy swells now hid the islands from us, now revealed them, and where Nordie and I chased the birds at sea and they talked to Amaru not with fingers but with wings. They knew more about fishing than I did, and almost as much as Nordie and Amaru.

Anecdotage

WHAT is a big fish? Why, I suppose it's a fish bigger than usual. Or as big as a particular kind of fish in a particular place is known to get, or somewhere near it. Or anyhow bigger than you or I have been in the habit of catching.

Why would a man rather catch a five pound pickerel in Pennsylvania than a twelve pound tuna at Block Island, a fifty pound tarpon in Florida, or a hundred and fifty pound shark anywhere? Because the pickerel is a big fish, and the others are not.

And also because he has known the one for a big fish ever since he was a boy, at which time the chances are the others had never swum into his ken. Moreover and in particular, I never did have the luck to land a five pound pickerel. But I've been after one all my life.

I want a big pickerel because I'm interested in pickerel. You can't interest a man very much in things for which he has no measure. The story of a big tarpon often leaves a trout fisherman cold. But tell him about a three pound trout in a brook he knows because he has fished it, and watch his eyes snap and his face shine.

Back in the old days in Pike County, before Big and Little Brink Ponds were changed into Twin Lakes and all mussed up with summer boarders, my brother Amos, Rob Hamilton, and I used to go there after pickerel, with the hope of a five pounder in the back of our minds.

We camped on the land of Monsieur de Rialp, a ballet

master most surprisingly domiciled far back in the wilds. Our tent was pitched by what was even then known as Silver Spring, because the white sand out of which it sprang made any other name impossible. We drank its waters, and we lived high. Not only pickerel, but the tribes of perch and sunfish yielded us of their abundance, and life was good at all points.

There was life in the water, and likewise living things on the land. One evening, just as dusk was turning to darkness, Rob Hamilton found a black rattlesnake near our tent, pursued it into the alders, and killed it with a piece of stick just half as long as the snake. He took a chance and got away with it.

That rattlesnake was good not only because Rob made it so with his abbreviated weapon, but after its decease. Rattlesnake meat is more like frog's legs than anything else, but if you should ask me how I know I would refuse to tell you.

The rattlesnake has its place in materia medica also. Old Jerry Greening happened around one day, Old Jerry whose wrist was as broad as two of mine, and who never wore gloves in the coldest winter. He told us of a sure cure for toothache.

"You ketch a rattlesnake alive," said he, "take him by the head with one hand and by the tail with the other, and nibble your teeth the length of his spine up and back, and if you bite him good you won't never have no toothache from that time on." Jerry lived on Rattlesnake Creek, and he had every chance to know. I was willing to take his word for it.

My father used to tell a story of a family that lived in Rattlesnake and yearly held a Christmas celebration. One very cold winter the celebration was especially enthusiastic

because a son who had been unavoidably detained by circumstances beyond his control was out and home again.

During the course of that convivial evening a difference
of opinion arose between this son and another, in the
progress of which one son bit off the other son's nose.
It was a regrettable occurrence, and something had to be
done about it. So they hitched up the cutter, and denosed
and denoser, amity restored, set out for the nearest doctor
with the amputated fragment and the laudable intention
of getting it sewed on again.

"But," said that member of the family who told my
Father about this social incident, "it warn't no use. The
damn thing froze."

There were lily pads in Big Brink Pond, and in the old
days you could anchor your boat just beyond them, catch
bait on one side with a little hook and a worm, and translate it into pickerel on the other. What fascination there
was in the movements of the cork, the quick and dainty
little jerks the live bait gave it, making the faintest ripples
on the still surface, the sudden yank when a pickerel
snatched the hook, the long suspense while he gorged it,
and then the smooth steady movement of the float as the
running fish drew it deeper and out of sight. Them was
the happy days.

Although none of us ever took the five pound pickerel
of our waking dreams, on one of those days Amos did
catch a pickerel that never felt the hook. Like a crab
with a piece of fish, this fellow hung on too long to a
deceitful shiner, and only dropped it when the net was
under him. Nine-tenths of wisdom is to be wise in time.

One afternoon my Mother and Father drove out to see
us, and on the way added one more rattlesnake to the
Pinchot history of Brink Pond. It got away in a stone-

wall, and left behind with both of them an incomprehensible prejudice against a region which to us youngsters was a land of pure delight.

Another evening (it was so long ago I don't remember whether the law forbade or not) Bob showed us how to spear pickerel by the light of a torch. It was new to me, and wonderful beyond description, to find that the clear water seemed to disappear, the boat to be suspended in the ether, and the fish satisfied to wait motionless for us to strike them. Today it's a forbidden pleasure, but I would love to do it again.

In those days, Brink Pond was eight miles away, over one of the worst roads the moon looked down upon. Each time we went there fishing, we made all ready the night before. We were up with the first gray dawn, and the sun rose over the eastern hills across the Delaware as the old horse took us slowly over ridge after ridge, the water dancing in the minnow bucket, while one of us held it and one of us drove.

Today you may reach Twin Lakes in your motor in fifteen minutes. But what a difference!

From Pickles to Molasses

"TOMORROW it will blow, but Friday the wind will probably moderate," said the official forecaster. And Friday it did. Saturday was one of those rare days when the beauty of the whole creation pierces almost to the dividing asunder of soul and spirit, when sea and sky amount to a visible thanksgiving, when a man cannot keep the words of the prophet out of his mind: "The whole earth is at rest, and is quiet; they break forth into singing."

A day of glassy calm on the Florida reef—there is nothing more serenely, more quietly glorious. It infolds and occupies a man's better nature, and seems to shut out all the world besides. Nevertheless, some few practical necessaries of life demand attention.

"First," said Captain Lowe, "we'll get some bait. Next we'll stop on Tavernier Shoal and see if we can't pick up the queen conchs you want for your boy. After that we'll run out to the reef, anchor the big boat, and work around in the tender. You take your water glass and I'll take mine, and we'll look the place over."

"You're the doctor," said I; and it was so ordered.

I put an end to a somewhat precarious tight-rope performance that had been going on during this conversation by climbing down from the slender stringers of the unfinished dock, jumped into the little tender, and we put-putted off to the crawfish grounds.

The inability of the crawfish tribe to get the meaning of two black points on a wooden handle descending slowly

The Nurse Shark Looks Different from in Front

through the clear water is a serious blot on their intellectual capacity. It appears to spring from a confidence men have done nothing to deserve, but it has very desirable consequences from the human point of view. Nevertheless, crawfishing with a pair of grains isn't always as easy as it looks, even with a glass-bottomed pail to help. That succulent hardshell has a habit of getting under whatever can be got under, and leaving nothing but his long whips sticking out to prove he's there but you can't get him. Before long, however, a half dozen spiny lobsters had been worked out of their holes in the coral, and that was enough for bait.

Then to the big boat—a launch less than thirty feet long—and in her to Tavernier Shoal, towing the tender. There we threw over the light anchor, took to the tender again, and with the captain poling in the bow and the writer observing in the stern, we moved against the conchs in solemn procession. In truth the pursuit of these exaggerated snails lacks somewhat in excitement, for their sole hope of escaping destruction is that no one who wants them will see them.

"There's a couple," said the captain. "Have you got the sponge hook? See if you can pick them out through the ripple." Which I did with some trouble, because of the sea growth which covered them, and then, with some more trouble, got the hook under each and deposited both in the bottom of the boat. They were thin-edged conchs, six or eight inches long, and far more active than I expected. One of them I laid on its back, and it actually succeeded in turning itself over with its sickle-shaped foot. That was new in my experience and a clear proof that I knew little of conchs.

"There's a queen conch right now," said the captain;

[95]

but it was a lamb conch, as the captain told me afterward. That one was easy to find—a huge and graceful shell swelling roundly in the middle and slender at both ends. It looked to be eighteen inches in length and certainly missed it but little. Two more queen or lamb conchs and a half a dozen of the smaller ones gave us all we wanted. There were too many of them to provide the hunt with even a moderate thrill. So we headed offshore, where the feeble remnant of yesterday's swell was flattening out every minute. It was perfect weather.

On Pickles Reef, where we anchored the launch again, the water was as limpid as a spring. Peace reigned, but the traces of tempest were all about us. This reef is marked by the wreck of an iron steamer loaded with cement in bags and in barrels, and both shapes, hard as stone, are still thickly scattered over the ocean floor, although cloth and wood have long since disappeared.

Here and there metal plates and girders strew the reef, and these we carefully visited in the tender. One triangular piece of wreckage that shows above the surface makes a sort of iron refuge for fishes. In and about this artificial cave, when we reached it, swam two of the most gloriously beautiful visions it has ever been my luck to see.

I have long known the blue-and-yellow angel fish, whose Spanish name is Little Isabel, and the ordinary undecorated black angel fish, but the black angel fish with deep gold rims on every scale of his broad side was new to me, and here were two of them. It was no trouble to attract the larger with some pieces of crawfish, and very little to get him to take a tiny hook into his tiny mouth. But it was a great deal of trouble, with a three-six rod and a six-thread line, to keep him out of his cave. Time and again he threatened to smash the only rod I had with me, or even break the line, for the angel fish, however deliberately he may swim when there is no excitement, is a very hard fighter. And this was a big one.

In the end, however, flax, bamboo and an educated thumb won over fish power and fish persistence, and at length I could lift this splendid creature from the clear still water into the clear still air. I laid him where I could see him, and looked and looked and looked. There is no use my trying to describe him—his black-brown side throwing the bright rims of each scale into brilliant relief, the two yellow spots like eyes on the top of his purple head, or all the rest of his glory.

But before long I had to choose between looking at him and letting him live, and so, by the long streamer of his dorsal fin, I lifted him carefully into the water again, and watched him swim away more and more swiftly, back into the darkness of his metal cave. His mate had disappeared.

Later I learned that I had caught and released a relatively rare fish, the French angel fish—Pomocanthus paru—but I loved him no better for that.

We hardly needed the two water glasses as we moved from one coral canyon to the next—smooth white coral sand on the bottom bearing the ripple marks the waves know how to make—overhanging walls of coral on each side, with here and there a living coral colony shaped like the fronds of a Japanese dwarf evergreen, but far larger, far more regular, and some of them far more lovely. And about the walls and the coral fronds, and over the sand, schools and flocks and herds and companies of fish which it is utterly beyond me to describe.

I have, and, if desired, could communicate, an idea of the gray background and brown markings of the Nassau groupers which lay on their sides on the sand and looked up at us through twenty feet of water, or stood on their tails to take note of the curious contraption that floated above them.

I could tell about the black groupers and certain huge parrot fish, with their black bodies and brilliant azure markings about the head. Some of them must have weighed twenty pounds. I could describe the yellow-tails, the grunts, the porkfish, the filefish, the big-eyed squirrel fish, the hinds, the tangs, and a lot of others, if I knew the names to which to attach my feeble effort to translate their beauty into cold type. But the impression made by the multitude of these gloriously beautiful creatures, the vividness and eccentricity of their coloring, and their violent contrasts with each other are far beyond my pen.

For the most part the fish we watched paid us not the slightest attention, but went about their fishy business as if we were in another world, as indeed we were. Unless we appeared to their untroubled eyes like mere black silhouettes against the brilliant sky, which seems reasonable, the ice-clear water and unwrinkled surface must have given them nearly the same chance to see us that we had to see them. They showed, however, little sign of modifying their behavior because of us, until a piece of crawfish floated down among them, free or on a hook. That changed their humor instantly, for crawfish meat is the best-loved morsel on the reef. That made the difference between loafing and getting a living—a living that might be very short indeed.

"If I bait this trap with crawfish," said the captain, speaking of a kidney-shaped woven-wire apparatus with an upward-pointing entrance in the middle of the concave side, "and let it down with my buoy line tied to it, not a Nassau grouper will go in; but if I leave the buoy line off they will. That isn't easy to believe, but I'll show you."

Easy to believe it certainly was not. I was willing to wait and see.

So down went the trap liberally baited with fresh amber-colored crawfish meat, buoy line attached—we would have better luck, said Captain Lowe, if the bait were only good and stale—and we went off to see more groupers, more angel fish, more parrot fish, more swarms of fish with wholly impossible colorings in one coral canyon after another along the length of the reef.

In half an hour or an hour—time was forgotten—we were back at the buoy. There was a big Nassau grouper outside the trap looking in, and a big black grouper inside the trap looking out. That was the first half of the proof. So far the buoy line had done precisely what the captain said it would.

It seemed impossible for so large a fish to get inside so small a trap, but there he was, and obviously most uneasy. Both groupers, captive and free, eyed us with the closest attention. And when the captain spliced the grains pole to another, hooked the grains into the wires, and began to lift, it was perfectly possible to see the increasing anxiety of the grouper in the trap as he neared the surface. His final panic as he reached the surface soaked us both liberally. That fish was very human.

As a game fish, the grouper may leave much to be desired. He bites, indeed, with ferocity, but being hooked his idea is not to run but to hide. Down he goes to the nearest rock and under it, and if you save him, it is either because no rocks are handy, or because your tackle is strong enough to let your engine tow him promptly out of the danger zone. It is as a personality that the grouper shines. He has a mind and uses it. The average angler holds him in less respect than he deserves.

"I want one of those Nassau groupers," said the captain. "They're the best eating fish on the reef. We'll set the trap again, drop the buoy a hundred yards away, and we'll see what's in it when we get back from the Beacon." Which we did accordingly.

By this time my back was nearly broken from stooping over my water glass and my knees were sore against the boat. But back and knees counted for little over against the keen excitement of this glorious day. What I wanted most of all was more of the same.

Molasses Beacon, two or three miles to the north of Pickles, stands on widespreading iron legs on top of the reef at the edge of the Gulf Stream. It is an automatic light. The sunlight is supposed to turn it off and the darkness to turn it on, but today it was sending out its flashes in the noonday. Thither we chugged away in the tender.

Before we had gone halfway a loggerhead turtle broke water close aboard. It was a lady turtle, and she was far too big to be taken into our fifteen-foot boat, even if we had wanted to grain her. So, with no hostile purpose, we turned and gave chase, just to see her close at hand in the radiant water. She did all her swimming with her front flippers, and used her hind legs only to steer. Her head was bigger than a football.

Clearly this turtle was no match in speed for the little tender, but clearly also, we were no match for her cunning. Every time we caught up to her she turned sharply, passed under the boat, and headed once more for the deep water; and each time we made the shortest circle we could and made after her again, only to see her fade at last into the deeper blue. Our good wishes went with her. I find I have less and less desire to kill as I grow older.

Molasses Beacon is white with the droppings of sea birds, and not an attractive roosting place for men. Fish love it. Around it just now were barracuda in swarms, as Captain Lowe had prophesied. Also, they were little ones, as he said they would be. Few of them were more than a yard in length. They paid no attention whatever to our efforts to catch them, partly because April is not their hungriest season, partly because they saw us all too clearly. Even when I caught and offered them a live yellowtail, they refused to be vamped.

But an oar moving in the water—that was another story. Curiosity was stronger than appetite. I had read many a time, especially in that great angling classic, Dr. Charles F. Holder's *Log of a Sea Angler,* that a barracuda will follow a sculling oar, fascinated by its motion. I was sure before that it was true. Now I am prepared to deal with the scoffer, scoff he never so loudly, for I have seen the thing myself.

For the barracuda I have small regard and smaller liking. I recognize that he fights on the surface, jumps, and is very swift and daring beyond other fish, and that he is more ferocious than the usual shark. All that is good—very good—from the point of view of a sea angler.

But his battle is short, and once in the boat he is slimy beyond anything but a gaff topsail cat, and he smells as if he needed a bath. I think of him always as a low-caste piratical fish—long, low, rakish, and heavily armed.

Scattered anywhere about his mouth are great teeth set fore and aft, and sharp as razors. These very teeth killed a young girl on the coast of Florida not long ago. Another girl, seeing her friend in trouble, swam out into the blood-stained circle and brought the victim in. For clear courage

I know of nothing to surpass that rescue.

I cannot tell how long or how far we floated over the corals and the sand and the illuminated fish of Molasses Reef. Time and distance had little place in that picture. But as we hung between two worlds of equal transparency, Captain Lowe discoursed on the nature of fishes.

"What is the name of that fish, captain?"

"That's a chub."

"Will he bite?"

"Yes, he'll bite, but you can't do anything with him on that three-six outfit. He'll go into a hole in the coral, and you'll lose him."

"How about that one?"

"That's a turbot. He'll bite and you can get him." Which he did and I did, by a narrow margin—and he weighed six or seven pounds.

"What are those?" as a school of blunt-nosed, fork-tailed fish surrounded the boat.

"Horse-eye jacks. You can't do anything with them, or with that mackerel either. It's too smooth and clear."

"How about that one?"

"That's a parrot fish. He won't bite." And he didn't. And so on, and so on. The fish did what he said they would as regularly as if they had their orders.

Captain Lowe knows the reef. He knows it because, with an observant mind, he has lived his whole life in its neighborhood. Man and boy, he has earned his living from the sea in Florida for nearly fifty years, and the weather and the water tell him what he wants to know. Soft-spoken and kindly, he is a fisherman born and bred, and he can rig a sailfish bait as well as ever I saw it done.

We drifted over a school of yellowtails, and I began to catch a few for bait. Pretty soon came a tremendous smash a hundred yards away. "I'll bet," said the captain, with some show of excitement, "that's an amber jack. Let's go and see."

So we sculled over in that direction, and, by George, there he was! And his mate with him.

"Put on a big hook quick," said the captain. "He'll take this yellowtail." And as I struggled with the clumsy fingers of frantic haste to make the change, the captain sculled ahead of the leisurely amber jack, who looked as if he weighed some forty pounds; and then, to my intense delight, got him interested in the oar just as the barracuda had been. This was a new fact. I had never run across it even in a book. Perhaps the interest of other big fish can be held in the same way. I intend to try it.

At length the big hook was ready. Over went the yellow-tail in the immediate vicinity of the amber jack, whom the oar had kept in the immediate vicinity of the boat.

One wiggle of the yellowtail that showed he was alive, and the next second the amber jack could not have con-solidated him more completely if he had been a small com-peting corporation.

I struck that amber jack as hard as my six-thread line made safe, but the proper response was lacking. The strikee failed to recognize the situation. More strikes, but the only result was a little half-hearted run, very much as a lazy old dog makes believe to chase a ball to please a child. So I kept on striking, and finally the truth prevailed, as it has a habit of doing, and the amber jack suddenly found him-self with an urgent engagement a long way off.

I was just settling down to what I regarded as a possible two-hour job—for a three-six outfit and a reel without a handle brake are not calculated for quick results with amber jacks—when somewhere in the distance the line grated across a bit of coral and the amber jack severed his connection with civilization and went his way, the richer by one yellowtail and six feet of wire with a perfectly good hook at one end and a perfectly good swivel at the other. What was left of the line came back to me.

There were too many incidents on that motionless but moving day to tell them all. Another turtle; a ten-foot shark waving his steady way under the boat; two black-and-white frigate birds, the most graceful and beautiful of all the sea birds I have known, and the uncanny accuracy with which one of them, a quarter of a mile in the air, delivered a bombing attack that did not miss the captain and the boat three feet; two young army officers who had come all the way out there in an old dory with an outboard motor and caught little for their pains, for this was a day to see fish and not to catch them.

And all the time the pervading impression of peaceful benevolence in sky and sea, with just a tinge of recollection of this same place as I saw it yesterday, white water all over it, and just a tinge of warning from the clouds piling up in the west. It was time to be moving.

And so back to Pickles Reef and the grouper trap through the still glorious and breathless afternoon. The buoy line being detached, this time the trap contained two Nassau groupers and a margate fish besides—which was the second part of the proof. The demonstration was complete. My hat was off to the captain and the groupers both.

The big Nassau that we wanted and had seen before had moved his comestibility elsewhere. One of those we did get was a light gray when he came out of the water, then changed in a moment to a strong mottling of brown, and then almost to black. Except in dolphins, I had never seen such rapid and striking color contrasts.

Then it came time to leave, for the squall which nearly always comes up after midday in such weather was moving in our direction. So to the big boat, up anchor, and away.

The rain struck us before we had gone a mile. It brought along wind enough to double the wetting power of the rain, but not enough to kick up any sea. I took refuge in the cabin, which the captain could not do. What soaking his slicker could not prevent he got, while I kept dry. And glad I was of it when he swung the boat around and headed back, for, said he, "This is about over and we can get another hour or two on the reef."

When we came again in the late afternoon to the iron cave of the black-and-gold angel fish, it held nothing beautiful, but instead the lumpish and almost formless figure of a toothless, harmless, stupid six-foot nurse shark, which made no move to escape, although we were squarely on top of it in less than five feet of water, until I began to discuss sticking a pair of grains into its almost impenetrable hide. Thereupon it departed.

The stillness after the squall was more marked than ever. No more looking through the water glasses. We saw fully without them. Here was another black-and-gold angel fish curving himself about the bastions of coral. He was even larger and more gorgeous than the first, but he refused to bite. Then a hogfish—misnamed, if ever a fish was—his long dorsal spines trailing behind him, bit promptly, but the coral cut the line.

A mutton fish, the biggest of a school, took the next bait. The water was so shoal and clear that I could see his eye as the bit of amber crawfish disappeared into his gray shape.

My little rod would have had its work cut out, but he fled under a natural bridge of coral and the line was severed.

A sting ray under a piece of the wreck, whom the grains

could not hold; a big Nassau grouper in shoal water, who got into a hollow coral head and watched us through a hole; and gray snappers, and still another turtle, and at every turn kinds of fish unseen before—it seemed as if there was no limit.

But all good times come to an end, as do all bad ones, and the moment came when we could tarry no longer. I hated to leave, of course—hated it like poison—but my cup was full, nevertheless. And so up anchor for the last time that day.

For a time there flew about us, and finally lighted on the tender, a little land bird with a black head and olive-green sides. What it was doing six or seven miles from shore, unless the squall had brought it, I couldn't imagine. It came with us a little way, and then flew off again. I fear it never reached the shore.

"Captain," said I, as he cleaned the Nassau groupers at the stern, "I noticed you thought little of that squall, or you would have gone in sooner."

"Well," said he, " when a squall is long in making up, there isn't much wind behind it. But if it makes up in a hurry, then watch out."

Which is contrary to the rule among humans, but a good thing for man who loves sea fishing to paste in his tackle box.

All the way in I watched the bottom change. First the reef, then clean coral sand, then the multicolored animal vegetation of the sea—sea fans and Venus' bathtubs and sea slugs looking like the curved gigantic fruit of some huge tree, and loggerhead sponges as big as barrels.

And as a fitting climax, a barracuda almost as long as I am flashed away from the bow. After such a day I was almost glad he wouldn't bite, but not without a mental reservation. Too much of this kind of good thing is just about right.

When the Dry Fly
Was New

(This story was written twenty-odd years ago. It is here printed just as it was written.)

I HAVE a classmate who has a brother who wrote a book. Therein he described what is at once the simplest and the most difficult, and by far the most attractive method of stream fishing that ever has come my way. The book is Emlyn Gill's *Dry Fly Fishing in America.* For me it opened the road to the most satisfactory of all forms of fresh water sport.

To read Gill's book was to be eager for the practice of the dry fly, so I sent to New York for the means, began with no teacher but the printed word, and dry fly fishing for trout captured me on the spot.

One of the charms of it is the simplicity of the outfit— a leader or two, a pill box with a few flies, a little one-drop oil can filled with albolene (five cents' worth of which will last you a season), and you have the whole of the special appliances necessary for the use of the dry fly beyond the ordinary equipment of rod and reel, creel and net.

Long before Emlyn Gill had come himself to teach me, by the example of the master at work, some of the finer points of dry fly fishing, I had discovered that it was possible, when streams were low, to take more and bigger fish with the dry fly than with the wet, and to take them not only in cloudy weather and at the two ends of the day, but in bright sunlight at noon, with the water clear as crystal, provided only you approach the trout from behind as he lies headed upstream, or otherwise keep out of sight.

There are two ways of staying hid. The one is to fish upstream with a long line delicately; the other to keep behind what cover there may be along the brook, so that the trout cannot suspect your presence, while you yourself often cannot see your fly as it takes the water. Each way is good in its place, but keep hid you must, except where the water is rapid. There, provided you fish upstream and your shadow is behind you, you may take trout almost between your feet.

In the Pennsylvania village where I live there is a man famous for years as the best fly fisherman of all that region. He knows the brooks as few men can, and the trout he has caught in past days make the envy and despair of his younger followers.

To him I said one day last summer, "Come to the Sawkill, and let me see you use the wet fly. I am studying trout just now, and I want to learn how you do it."

"No," said he, "this is a bad day. When the brooks are low, I must have cloudy weather. I will call you up the first good day."

So he did, and we went to the stream at the time and place he chose. But the water was still too low for the wet fly, and he had no sooner seen the brook than he said so; and he added, "I can do nothing in this water. Let me see you try."

Just then a trout rose in a long still reach of the stream. There was no cover near, and the rise was nearly as far from where we stood as the longest cast I could manage.

But by good fortune reach it I did (I am a very moderate fisherman) and the response was satisfactory. By the time the trout had got his liberty again (for this was a native trout, and since, worse luck, there are brown trout in this brook, for the present all the natives caught go back), the veteran's ideas began to undergo a change.

On our way to the brook he had condemned the dry fly without mercy. Now he had seen taken a trout which the wet fly could not possibly have reached. To make the story short, throughout the afternoon the wet fly took no fish, while the dry fly made a score of eight, four of which, being natives, were returned to the stream.

My friend went home converted, but not before he had promised that some day when the stream is high he will show me how the Cahill fly (which bears his name) will do its work under his hand in roily water.

Another day another friend of mine—Grant, we will call him because that happens to be his name—was walking up the Sawkill with me about the middle of a hot still afternoon. The brook was excessively low, the water clear as glass, but what little wind was stirring came from the South, and here and there a trout was rising. As we came near the spring by which we meant to eat our belated lunch, we saw, holding his place almost without motion in the imperceptible current, a brown trout well over a foot long.

He was lying in water not two feet deep, close behind a high tuft of grass upon the bank, and he rose as we watched him, and saw us as he rose. It would have been useless to "chuck a brute of a fly" at him just then.

"We'll attend to him after lunch," said Grant, and on we went to the lunching place. But all the while we were lunching we could see that our fish was lunching too. We finished eating, my friend smoked his smoke out to the end, but evidently the fish was hungry still.

Finally Grant could stand it no longer. Crawling on hands and knees, as though he were stalking big game, as indeed he was, Grant reached the cover of the bunch of grass. Once there, the trout was within ten feet. There had been no jarring footfall, no movement of grass or brush, and the trout was still unfrightened and unaware. Then the single fly dropped delicately upon the water above the feeding fish, which did not wait for this final course of his long meal to be brought slowly to him by the stream, but came swiftly to meet it.

There followed as pretty a fight as you will often see. Three times the brown trout came out of water with a rush, and it was not until after a most spirited struggle of ten minutes that the net rose round him—a beauty 15 inches in length, and a pound and a half in weight.

This fish represented the best size and condition of brown trout rising to the dry fly in this particular stream. Here was a fish, wholly inaccessible to the wet fly as such, and which the longest and finest casting even of the dry fly might well, in such a place and on such a day, have frightened and put down. It was taken purely because the fish did not know the fisherman was about.

Someone may say that, in this particular instance, a grasshopper would have answered the purpose just as well. It is possible, although not probable, but this much is certain, that in such a case the pleasure of the recollection would have lost its finest quality.

For me, two trout stand out as the best catches of that season. One of them was the last I took, a fish of a pound and five ounces. As I walked quietly at sunset through the old meadow along the brook, it rose with a splash. The rise I heard but could not see till the widening ripples had

Where the Big Ones Rise at Evening

half crossed the stream. Then, lengthening my line from behind some bushes, I cast around them, so that the fly struck the water out of my sight. Up came the trout smartly, and I hooked him by the sound of his rise.

I was fishing with perhaps thirty feet of line, and for the moment that was all I had, because the rest of it, to my shame, was tangled on the reel. Also, I was on my way home and fishing, as I seldom do, downstream, and downstream went the trout when I hooked him. He had to be stopped short, for there was no more line to give him, and stopped he was, and out of the water he came, and the leader held, and at the end of five minutes of vigorous play the net rose round him too, and I had finished the season with one of its finest fish.

The best of the English dry fly fishers are, I am told, the purists, who will cast at a trout only after they have seen him rise. If the trout are not rising, there is no fishing, and not only the fly but the line goes home as dry as it came out. We in America fish streams less known, less clear, less placid, and we are always speculating, dropping the dry fly here and there where a trout is apt to be, seeking our luck from the stream even though no trout rises to invite us to come and kill him.

I am by no means a purist. I am given to taking chances along the brook; but the more I fish with this most sport-giving of entanglements the more I find myself enjoying the taking of the individual fish that I have seen and stalked and hooked, as against the promiscuous unseen fish I have cast for merely in general.

There is a spot in a meadow brook where two logs cross. Near them lie the last remnants of an ancient beaver dam, and these, it is reported, are inhabited by huge and somewhat legendary trout whose weight and length and game qualities may be set as high as the reader pleases. I wish I knew. Coming home one evening at the heel of a rather unsuccessful day, between dog and wolf, as the French say, just when the beauty of the brook is at its loveliest, I saw the second of my two best trout rise in the angle of the logs.

The distance was about the limit of my casting power, which is not set at ninety odd feet like Emlyn Gill's, but at a figure so much more modest that it declines to be mentioned at all. Luck was with me, and when at last the line was well out, the whirling dun dropped lightly in the angle. Instantly came the strike, and instantly the hooked trout dove under and between the logs. It was a ticklish moment, with so much line out, but the tangle became untangled, the roots and branches were cleared, and one of the most welcome trout I ever caught came to the nearer bank.

It was not the legendary big fellow, but only a trout of a pound. Yet because I had seen him and gone after him, had fished for him perfectly so far as my abilities would take me, and had landed him without a mistake, that fish makes, and will continue to make, one of the pleasantest memories of my days along the brook.

There is no question, I take it, that the dry fly beats the wet fly when streams are low, and I judge from my small experience that at all times the average of fish taken is larger with the dry fly than with the wet. Indeed, there are but three things to be said in even partial detraction of it.

The first is that the dry fly requires a far more intimate knowledge of the places where fish lie, and of their habits of feeding than does the wet fly. The brown trout, for example, on clear sunny days with the wind in the South, affects the lower margins of still pools, lying many times on sand bars in six or eight inches of water, plainly visible to the distant but discerning fisherman, yet out of reach of all but the most careful casting of the dry fly. At such times, let your fly drop six feet to one side and a little behind the fish, and if he has not seen you, which he can do at the most astonishing distances and through the most astonishing amount of cover, you are more than likely to hook him, and to find him of good size.

At other times you will get no fish but in the riffles, and yet again only in the deepest center of the pools, at which times the dry fly jerked under and retrieved below the surface has a fascination often not to be denied. So this first objection is really an advantage, for the dry fly compels you to learn your fish.

The second detraction is that dry fly fishermen are the natural prey of all the brush along the streams. The need of false casts to dry the fly makes so many additional opportunities for all the prehensile fingers of the trees to snatch your hook, and the fact that you must fish against the current, and therefore cannot trust it to place the fly for you, makes longer casting, with a good back cast, most necessary. In other words, the dry fly requires a kind of handling of the rod and line on wooded streams which adds ten fold at times to the aggravation, and on those rare occasions when everything a man does goes well, a hundred fold to the delights, of the fishing.

This second drawback then is really but a spur to ambition in disguise. Nevertheless, if you own the stream, use your axe where the brush is thickest. You will be astonished at the comfort which will follow a little judicious cutting.

The third difficulty is more serious. Accuracy in the placing and management of the fly is more essential to success with the dry than with the wet fly, of which latter I speak as a user and lover for many years; and accuracy in the placing and handling of the fly involves a degree of eye strain, especially if a very small fly be employed, which may amount to a serious drain upon the angler. This is the one real objection to dry fly fishing.

There is a pool upon the Sawkill where in the edge of the evening you may see and hear trout rising with the deep convincing plop which always means a heavy fish. I have haunted that pool evening after evening, when the colors of sky and land and water were almost enough to drown the love of fishing. I have cast my longest and finest. I have done my very prettiest. I have dropped my fly over the rising trout just beyond the grass, and in the center just below the middle of the rise. Evening after evening I have come back from that pool with my trouble for my pains.

I have used the whirling dun and Wickham's fancy, the most uniformly successful flies upon that brook, and the coachman, the pale evening dun, the Cahill, and many another fly whose name I do not know; and night after night those fish rise and rise, but not for me; and night after night I go home without them.

What ever it is they feed on they will take within six inches of my fly, but my fly they do not strike. Gill has tried them; Grant has tried them; my brother has done his best. We are not good enough, yet. We do not know how, yet. Could there be a stronger reason for the preparations which are already under way for the next season's campaign?

The Sharks of Bone Key

THE one best recipe for carrying responsibilty easily
is not carry it all the time. The spring whose tension
is never released must weaken, and the man who thinks
about nothing but work is inevitably consumed by it. In a
sense, our best work is done in play time.

But how shall an outdoor man shift the burden when he
can not get outdoors? How shall he slip out from under
the weight and the strain of the things for which he is
responsible when the woods and the waters are not acces-
sible to him, when he must keep on living in town? Obviously by reading books about fishing. That is my own
prescription and practice, and I commend it to others. It
was purely to supply the drug needed for filling this prescription that the present book was undertaken.

The dean of the sea anglers' fraternity, as all good fishermen know, was Doctor Charles F. Holder. I believe I
could pass a rigid examination in nearly everything he has
ever written, and in particular in what he has told us about
the Florida keys,—stories so vivid and delightful that for
me they have made a new wonderland, with a glamour
which even personal contact can not dispel—a rare quality
in wonderlands, and greatly to the Doctor's credit.

One of the passages which I remember best is the story
of the sharks at the slaughter house in Key West. So,
when I came at last to that Havana-filled town where
Cubans roll cigars, my strongest impulse was the desire for

a visit to the Holder-hallowed slaughter house and the catching of a Holder-hallowed shark.

Dr. Mayer, head of the Tortugas Biological Laboratory, and I were on our way there, and if you want to know what he thought about sharks you will find it on another page of this casual chronicle. Meantime the catching was not difficult—an open launch, a trailing skiff, a friend, a boatman, and a Conch, and the thing was done.

To him who does not know, it may be said that a Conch is a native Floridian, whose business or quasi-business takes him on the water. The Conch in question was shiftless, thin, unreliable, brick-color, and avaricious, but he certainly showed us sharks.

On the southerly shore of Cayo Hueso, which being interpreted is Bone Key, but which has now become transmogrified into Key West, stands the historic slaughter house. Seaward its doors open over a wall set in 4 or 5 feet of water, and there the refuse is thrown out, to be disposed of by the sharks.

When we arrived our Conch asked a couple of negroes who were washing down the floor whether the sharks had been about that morning. They said they had, and that a few minutes ago a big black fellow had been in sight. They complained, further, that the sharks used to come right up to the sea wall for their food, but now at times they were compelled to "haul it out to 'em in a boat." Then suddenly one of them pointed: "There he is now."

Now as to sharks I am purely orthodox. All my life I had been accustomed to associate sharks with a sinister triangular fin cutting sharply through the water, whose burnished surface hid the grisly shape beneath, and in this I am well fortified by all the best literature. In the present case, however, I could see no fin, and for a time could see no shark. Afterward I had no trouble.

Under the advice of the Conch, we anchored in 8 or 10 feet of the clearest water, over a white sand bottom against which a minnow two inches long would have been clearly visible. Then we baited the hooks, first with refuse from the slaughter house, and later with pieces of fish, and waited. It seemed an incredible place to fish for sharks.

The white sand of the bottom was cut, parallel to the shore, by long somber bands of rocks, which replaced the sand altogether where the water deepened to 15 or 20 feet. Presently, a faint discoloration appeared over the dark rocks, and then there swam deliberately across the bright white sand a black sharp-edged shadow, which was a shark. The brute (I call him so advisedly, for his disposition was most unaccommodating) seemed enormous. Slowly he moved back and forth from rock to sand and from sand to rock, working the whole region in our neighborhood as a bird dog works a field; all of it, that is to say, except where the bait lay. Then he disappeared.

Shortly afterward, so clear was the water and so white the sand, we sighted another shadow more than a hundred yards away, and coming in our direction. The tension began all over again. Would this shark bite? Questing he came on, struck the scent, worked back and forth across the trail until he found the bait, held all our sympathetic attention while he examined it with painstaking particularity, and went away.

Then we decided that the bait on the white sand was too conspicuous, and we moved it over to the rocks. Again came the shadow, smaller this time, yet enormous still, again the search and the finding of the bait, but this time the bait was taken and the shark was hooked. As soon as the line began to run out I jumped into the dingy with the Conch, and when we were clear of the launch I struck. Off went the shark with a vigorous rush, and off went the boat behind him. But this was relatively a small fish, but 6 feet 6 inches long, and held out not more than ten minutes against the hickory rod and 24 thread line. Then I shot him, as all good fishermen do, and the bait was set again for the next.

Hardly had this first shark been caught and disposed of when one of the lines fouled on a rock, and it looked as if we might have to break it. Thereupon the Conch began to take off his shirt. We inquired of him with some curiosity what he was doing, and he replied that he proposed to swim out and clear the line. We said that there was a dingy alongside admirably adapted to that purpose, which hint made no impression upon his mind at all.

Whether it was valor, pride, the desire to impress the tenderfoot, or a keen sense of the possible effect upon his stipend, we shall never know, but we had almost to hold that Conch in the boat to keep him from going overboard. I presume it would have been safe enough. Evidently he thought so. Men go overboard freely from docks at Key West off which sharks as heavy as a horse are caught at night. Personally, however, the boat was good enough for me just then, so I took the dingy and freed the hook.

About this time the contemplative calm which is supposed to brood over all fishing was violently interrupted by two Cuban brothers in a skiff. The brother in the bow was using the grains; the brother in the stern was using the paddle, and both were using their vocal chords without economy, pause, or delay. I have often heard that fish do not mind talking. Certainly Florida fish do not, for otherwise every fin within a mile would have been aware of that skiff and outward bound. Its occupants were after what they could get and a good time,—and a good vociferous time they were certainly getting.

While waiting for the sharks we had seen several of the beautiful whiprays, or calico fish, floating past over the white bottom, and we called the attention of the skiff to one of them. Thereupon the brother in the bow did a workmanlike job, for he struck the whipray with the grains in not less than six feet of water. He had, however, neglected to fasten a rope to his weapon. Off went the ray with the grains in its back; off went the skiff after the grains, the Cuban brothers poling and paddling in a frenzy of haste, and bow and stern yelling, "Git 'im, Git 'im," nineteen to the dozen.

To say that it was a scene of frenzied excitement is a scandalous understatement. Up and down the coast went the ray, and up and down the coast after him went that boatload of howls and yells, until the grains were recovered, the whipray was landed, and we had bought it for two bits as a subject for dissection at the Tortugas Biological Laboratory. It was cheap at the price.

During this episode there were no sharks about. Shortly after came two, the largest we had seen. It was the smaller of the pair that took my bait, this time on a 36-thread line I had brought with me especially for large sharks. The line ran out without a click, for the big reel does not carry one (as it should), and the Conch and I jumped into the dingy. Then I struck, and struck, and struck again, till I was sure that shark was hooked.

The strike was followed by a short sharp run, and that by another, until perhaps 100 yards of line had been taken out, and the boat, stern-first, was running fast through the water and diagonally out to sea. It was hard work while it lasted, but within half a mile the rushes were checked, the fish under control, and we started back, for I did not want to kill the shark until we were near the launch again. In 23 minutes from the strike the .45 Colt had done its work and the fish was dead.

This shark was carrying about with it several Remoras, one of which, over two feet in length, hung about the body of our first catch as it lay in the bottom till I caught it with a little hook. The shark itself, a female, measured 56 inches in girth behind the fins, and 108 inches in length. By the old formula, (the square of the girth in inches, multiplied by the length in inches, divided by 800), it weighed 422 pounds. I should have liked to see what could be done with the larger one. A 36-thread line, if you have enough of it and a Murphy hickory rod, is almost tackle to catch whales.

The next was a seven-foot shark caught by Doctor Mayer on a hand line, and then came lunch—lunch preceded by a swim in the breast-deep water, where even these beach-combing sharks would not be likely to come. If some one had begun to sing:

"God save you, merry gentlemen,
Let no shark you annoy"

it would have reflected my profoundest aspirations. But Dr. Mayer didn't care at all.

I kept my eyes well open, for against the brilliant sand the sharks we had seen looked simply gigantic, and the impression of weight and power was well confirmed by those we caught. I never have liked the idea of being consolidated, in whole or in part, with one of these buzzards of the sea. Most of them, I doubt not, are harmless enough, but you can never tell. All of them are heavily armed. Even the most dangerous species doubtless lose much of their dangerous quality when well fed, and the rarity of authenticated cases of shark bite indicates how small is the risk.

Yet the mental picture of that spasmodic snapping bite, so well calculated for the dividing asunder of whatever falls between the jaws, has for me most of the outstanding qualities of the dream of a rarebit fiend. They may be harmless. You never can tell. So far as sharks are concerned, I am firmly persuaded it is better to be safe than to be sorry.

Sharks are far more common than we are apt to suppose. Years ago I spent two summers on the south shore of Long Island. My chief delight was then a Peterboro canoe, in which another boy and I spent many a happy halfday running out through the surf and running in again, the percentage of upsets varying with the amount of sea. Because we ran out in this way we soon learned that outside the bathing beach swam a constant procession of small sharks, hammerheads and others, few if any of them more than 5 or 6 feet in length, harmless without question, but abundantly sufficient to have filled the bathers with panic had their presence been known. What kept them there, a few hundred feet from shore, I do not know, but I do know that day after day we saw them, and day after day we hunted them with a lily iron, fit only for much larger game, with which we struck many but caught none.

Is a shark game? In my experience, the shark of 100 pounds or under usually makes a good fight, often in no wise inferior to that of a tarpon of the same size so far as power and ginger are concerned, and many of them jump from the water almost as finely. If you can get a good fight out of a shark, why not take it and enjoy it, and be thankful for what the Wet Gods provide?

Doubtless the larger sharks are usually slow and heavy,

but some of them are, and all of them look, savage enough to overbalance any lack of fire. Besides, every time you kill a shark, it is a good deed shining in a naughty world. Where can you find a virtue more pleasant in practise?

There is joy in the catching but not in the killing of a trout. If you must keep him for the pan, well. If you can return him to the stream, to fight again another day, better. But there is no substratum of regret when you kill a shark. If the sight of his teeth is not enough, take but one glance at his eye, and every vestige of pity dies. A shark's eye is its own death warrant, and in all good conscience you can do nothing less than carry the warrant out.

Doubtless, too, sharks are vermin in the same sense that a rat, a weasel, a wild cat, a mountain lion, and a Bengal tiger are vermin. Dangerous vermin, some of them, like some sharks, and well worth hunting, but vermin still. Yet if a game fight makes a game fish, I have caught many sharks that were truly game, and I confess to an inextinguishable delight in fighting and destroying them.

Solomon in Scales

THIS fish story is under the patronage and protection of the Department of Marine Biology of the Carnegie Institution of Washington. If you will look in Volume II of the Papers from the Tortugas Laboratory of the said Institution on page 257 thereof, *et seq.,* you will find it camouflaged, concealed, and hidden away under the title: An Experimental Field-Study of Warning Coloration in Coral Reef Fishes, by Jacob Reighard, Professor of Zoology in the University of Michigan.

When you have read the report you will see that this story is clearly impossible and beyond belief. Yet Jacob tells it with such calmness and such convincing columns of figures and such back, front, and side lights, and with such pictorial illumination, and is so sublimely unaware of what a good thing he's got, that you can't somehow help but believe his tale, although nothing like it has been seriously asserted since the beginning of the world. Anyway I am not responsible. Address all complaints to the Carnegie Institution, Washington, D. C.

Sixty miles west from the southern extremity of Florida lie the Dry Tortugas, as many little patches of sand as the hurricanes choose to leave above water. On one of them, Loggerhead Key, is the Government lighthouse and the Marine Laboratory of the Carnegie Institution. On another, Garden Key, stands the beautiful and massive masonry of Fort Jefferson, built at the close of the Civil War as a refuge for our fleet in the Gulf of Mexico, but now abandoned. The other keys rise but a few feet out of water, are mere heaps of sand, but the shallows and the channels which lie between and around them make up one of the most attractive fishing grounds I know.

It is the purpose of the Tortugas Laboratory to find out about any living thing that has its being in salt water. In pursuit of this eminently laudable object, it desired to discover what place color might have as an influence upon the feeding habits of a fish common in those parts, the Grey Snapper (Luteanus griseus). The Snapper feeds mainly on a fish about two inches long called a hardhead. Underneath the dock of the Tortugas Laboratory on Loggerhead Key lived the colony of Grey Snappers that supplied the raw material of the experiment which gave rise to this super-veracious tale.

As a sort of curtain raiser to the main inquiry, hardheads alive and dead were first thrown to the Snappers. They ate both indifferently. Then hardheads, dead of course, were dyed red, yellow, green, blue, and purple, and thrown to the Snappers, which ate 'em all without prejudice.

Then (and here it seems as if perhaps the Society for the Prevention of Cruelty to Animals ought to have been called in) individual hardheads were filled full of formaldehyde, formic acid, quinine, quinine and red pepper, red pepper alone, ammonia, and even carbon bisulphide, the motive power of the deceased egg, and thrown to the Snappers. The Snappers ate 'em all.

This experiment having proved conclusively that the Snapper and the human differ in their tastes as to condiments in food, hardheads denatured in various ways were submitted—as for example, by cutting sections out of a hardhead and sewing the abbreviated fish together, by sewing three fish together in the form of a triangle, and by decorating the departed hardheads with pieces of string up to more than a foot in length. The Snappers ate 'em all.

Finally certain red dyed hardheads had tentacles of Medusa, a stinging jellyfish, introduced into their mouths. This was different. By the time 178 of these Medusa-tentacled hors d'oeuvres had been eaten by about 150 Snappers, the lesson had been learned—red hardheads were unpalatable. The Snappers refused to touch any more of them. They continued to accept blue and yellow and unstained hardheads with the same cheerful voracity as before, but the reds were taboo.

Now comes the snapper of this Snapper story. These experiments with the jelly-fished hardheads closed on July 19, 1907. Twenty days later, on the eighth of August, red, white, blue, and yellow hardheads were thrown, mingled together, to the same Snappers under the dock. The white were taken, the blue absorbed, the yellow gathered in, every last one of them, but the red were absolutely refused. The Grey Snappers actually remembered the fact that red hardheads were poor eating. Blues and yellows and whites were welcome, but red hardheads—No.

And not only those remembered that had eaten the unpalatable red hardheads, but also those that had not, for it is not to be supposed that every individual of the colony of 150, big and little, got one of the 178 Medusa-ed minnows. These also, with one accord, recalled after twenty days that a fish of one special color out of several artificial tints had disagreeable properties—properties of which they had learned, however, not through their own personal experience, but only through the experience of other fish.

Color discrimination, intercommunication, memory! Let him who can match this story throw the first stone.

The Dry Tortugas are forty miles from the nearest land.

They are without a mangrove swamp to breed mosquitoes, without a telephone, a telegraph, or a postoffice, without a human habitation except those I have described. My visit to this perfect spot I owe first to Doctor Holder's writings, which made me thirst to go there, and next to Doctor Alfred G. Mayer, then Director of the Tortugas Biological Laboratory, who invited me to quench that thirst.

It was one of my most successful fishing trips, yet I took few fish. Perhaps a dozen small barracuda, some of which astonished me by coming out of water like tarpon, a single tarpon strike, an angelfish or two, a few grunts and yellowtails, a muttonfish, a schoolmaster, and a few small sharks, and then the Grey Snappers.

Life at the Dry Tortugas was the finest combination of simple living and high thinking that has ever fallen to my lot. Up at sunrise and into the glorious blood-warm water of the Gulf before breakfast. Then a day as full of interest as an egg is of meat, and after supper a walk with Doctor Mayer down to the end of the island, to consider the state of the universe and the habits of the Grey Snapper.

But if there is little human society on the Dry Tortugas (although what there was was of the very best when Doctor Mayer was in residence), there are abundant compensations. Thus the birds, for one key at least, go far to supply the interest unfeathered bipeds might be expected to bestow. Bird Key harbors a most remarkable community of noddies and sooty terns. The terns lay their single eggs on the sand; the noddies, whose name comes from their punctilious courtesy in bowing to each other when either mate returns to the nest, build for their future children rude supports in the bushes a foot or two from the ground.

According to the stories, all the way from King Solomon to Bellevue Hospital, human mothers have been known to

The Barracuda's Teeth Can Kill

mix their babies or have them mixed. Then what about the innumerable feathered mothers in a rookery—not only when their youngsters are visible in something dimly approaching their final form, but when they are still invisible in the egg? How does a tern know which of 10,000 eggs laid on the bare sand is her own and not her neighbors when there isn't a nest or a bit of sea weed or even a cross to mark the spot?

The answer seems to be an impossibly keen sense of locality. Doctor John B. Watson, of Johns Hopkins University, who has since become famous as the propounder of Behaviorism, told me about it. Attired in nothing whatever but a magnificent coat of tan, he came sailing in to Bird Key one day when I happened to be there. The lighthouse keeper's wife, the only woman in the group being on another Key altogether, his Tortugas costume in no way disturbed his academic calm.

Doctor Watson said something like this: He caught a tern on her nest, banded the bird and marked the egg, then turned the bird loose and moved the egg a few inches. The tern mother came back and claimed it. But when the egg was moved as much as fifteen inches, it was no longer within the purview of her maternity, and she assumed that it belonged to somebody else.

Fifteen inches displacement to the side meant an orphaned egg. But displacement in height had no such effect. An egg reposing on a platform twelve feet high, but mathematically centered over the spot on which it had reposed twelve feet below, continued to be recognized, and claimed as though it were still lying just where the lady laid it.

I suppose that some such miraculous accuracy as this is indispensable and inevitable in dense colonies of nesting birds where the eggs must lie close together. And I suppose it must be connected also with the equally miraculous and equally necessary sense of direction which these birds possess. For how else could a tern get home through a dense fog after flying miles and miles to sea? But the achievement is by no means the less marvelous for that.

Doctor Watson took some of the banded sea birds, put them in cages shut in with canvas against any view of their surroundings, shipped them by boat to Key West, and then by train far back into the mainland. Certainly birds turned loose under these circumstances, if they could be lost at all, ought to be lost hopelessly.

Yet twenty-four hours was long enough to get most of them back to the Dry Tortugas, and to their individual eggs.

I have known woodsmen who could make a circle of miles in a dense and pathless forest, come back to the individual tree from which they started, reach round it, and pick up the stick they had leaned against it on the side from which they started. But they had their eyes open and their feet on the ground. We humans have not evolved to where we are without losing powers that might be very useful on occasion.

But let's re-tern to our feathered muttons. Terns and noddies are respectable householders and good citizens, but they no more than humans, are immune from the powers that prey. It was indeed hardly to be expected that all this potential food in the form of eggs and birds should not be fed upon. There is (or was) a hawk which floated across once or twice a day from the fort and took a tern or a noddie for its meal, to the despair of Doctor Watson, whose special care and study the birds were.

There was also a colony of laughing gulls upon another key, a few of which would come over (until they lost their interest in tern eggs by the shot-gun route), stick his or her bill into the egg which pleased the fancy, carry it to the edge of the water (for what reason I cannot imagine), and there break it and eat it, so that high-water mark on the lee shore was dotted with egg shells for a hundred yards.

Then there were the frigate birds, dozens of them, on the wing well nigh the most beautiful of flying things, but at rest on the island altogether too much like long-bodied long-tailed turkey buzzards. A frigate bird ought never to touch the earth except in the darkest night, for to see one perched is to lose respect for it altogether.

I'm not so sure of that now as I was when I wrote it. Since then I have walked up to frigate birds on their nests in the Galapagos and other South Sea Islands, and have stroked their shining backs, and opened out their folded wings, and handed them pieces of fish, all of which they accepted as if to be fed and fondled by a perfect stranger was their ancestral right. Perhaps their tameness predisposed me in their favor. At any rate the ugliness I thought I saw before had disappeared.

The frigates of the Tortugas, like the hawks and gulls, preyed on the noddies and terns, but they were too rare, and when in the air too glorious, for any reasonable being to think of shooting them. But though immune they were not popular. Therefore Doctor Watson and I contrived a plot against them, with a strictly scientific purpose in the foreground. We proposed to catch a frigate, see whether his performance matched his appearance, and specifically how many pounds weight his great spread of wing would enable him to lift and fly away with.

Our first plan was to approach the roosting birds at night behind the glare of an electric torch, and so pick them off the bushes before they knew what we were after. But the moon spoiled that. The birds saw us as well as they saw the lights and removed themselves accordingly.

Now I confess that this particular method of capturing a frigate bird was regarded by me with hesitation. The frigate has a habit of snapping his bill, and when he does the sound of it can be heard down wind for several hundred yards. It has a bang like the shot of a small pistol, and the longer you think about it the bigger the pistol gets. Although not necessarily fatal, such a bite might be deucedly unpleasant. So doth the unknown make cowards of us all. I have since survived a bite from a frigate on my finger without even an abrasion of the cuticle. It was all sound and fury, signifying nothing.

When cunning (with a torch) had failed, we fell back upon force. The frigate bird, like many other birds of great cruising radius, rises into the air with difficulty, and often must face the wind to rise at all. By charging with the wind we thought it might be possible to make a frigate leave his perch in the same direction and seize him, thus handicapped, before he could take the air again. It seemed a reasonable plan.

Accordingly, having crept as near as we could get under cover of the brush and the darkness, through the shrieking swarms of terns and noddies, like children in a hailstorm, we rushed down wind upon the roosting frigates. We hoped that in the excitement at least one frigate bird would leave his perch with the wind instead of against it. And it happened even so.

We caught one frigate, to find not only that his bite was harmless, but that the whole creature, so great and splendid in the air, weighed little more than a good sized broiler. The disillusionment was bitter, and moreover there was egg on our shoes—lots of egg.

Black Bill, the Bird Buccaneer, was only meant to look at. Upon this observation I might philosophize at length. Anyhow, we put Bill in a dark room to spend the night while we slept off our disappointment. The next day, with much travail, we made for him a most careful harness which would distribute the weight of his scientific experimental burden without hampering his wings. Then we dressed him up in it, attached the s. e. burden to the harness, which in plain English was a little bag of sand, tied a line to him, and flew him from a fishing reel.

But Bill was a continuous flop. His ferocity had disappointed us, his weight had disappointed us; now we found that in spite of his spread of wing (about seven feet) his carrying capacity was but little over a pound. So we told him what we thought of him and turned him loose.

He left us, I think, without regret. We watched him rise into the air and shake himself like a hen emerging from a dust bath and rise again, shake himself once more till his feathers were clean of us, and then sail quietly back to where we caught him. I am almost inclined to wish we had let Black Bill alone.

In this environment the first Grey Snappers I saw were around the coral heads, great rocky mushrooms, a few of which still remain in the shallow water near the Laboratory. Deep, sturdy, knowing-looking fish they are, usually from three to five pounds in weight, although I understand that occasionally they reach several times that size. The coral heads, often 15 feet in diameter, are divided by countless passages and crevices in which the yellowtails, the Grey Snappers, and many other fishes literally swarm. I saw the Snappers too around the old iron wreck which lies about two miles westward from the lighthouse on

Loggerhead Key. Wherever I saw them I tried to catch them. And wherever I tried to catch them I failed. I had heard that the Snapper was the cunningest fish of the reef. Before long I was willing to swear to it.

Now as Doctor Mayer and I went about the Island he told me many stories of his experiences, his experiments, and the purposes of his work, and among other things he told me the story of Grey Snappers I have just told you. But he was far from stopping there. He said he had an escort of Grey Snappers which often kept pace with him in the water as he walked along the beach at night. And furthermore, he said I could see them if I wanted to.

I certainly did and so would you. So Mayer and I walked along the beach one brilliant moonlight night to see. And the escort of Snappers appeared according to schedule, as it were keeping step with us in the very edge of the sea.

They had, it appeared, discovered that when a man walks the beach at night the little grey spirit crabs scatter ahead of him into the edge of the waves. They knew already that spirit crabs are good to eat. Putting which two and two together, they trailed along in the water, keeping abreast or just ahead of the walking humans, and harvested the wages of their wisdom as the crabs transferred themselves from our jurisdiction into theirs.

So absorbed were the Snappers, and so bold, that they pushed themselves into water too shallow for upright swimming, and flopped on their sides where the ripples broke. It seemed as if they would certainly strand themselves for good and all. In their eagerness they made a sucking noise like German carp—which was neither pretty nor polite. I hate a carp anyhow.

I was lost in wonder and delight, as any lover of fishes

[132]

must have been, but little by little I began to think. I had failed to make Grey Snappers take the hook by day— but at night they would take crabs. The bearing of this incident surely lay in the application of it. To a man who had been fishing for Snappers and catching none, the lesson was plain as a pike-staff.

Most of the next day I spent digging out spirit crabs. The spirit crab lives in a hole in the sand, but when he is out of it, there is nothing swifter that travels the earth except possibly Malcolm Campbell, and I am not even sure about that. Greased lightning is leisurely by comparison. The only way for a man to catch a spirit crab is to chase him into his hole and then dig him out of it, or drive him into the water and grab him there.

The next evening found me prepared, in the matter of spirit crabs, to use the information the Snappers had given me. And their tip was good. They lived up to their promises. They bit as fast as my crabs struck the water, and they fought like higly intelligent tigers against the spring of my little rod. When I excavated those crabs I had struck pay dirt at last.

I was fishing with a 5-piece 5-ounce Leonard valise fly rod and a single-action Leonard reel. They had been my companions for many years all over the United States. They had taken kingfish, Spanish mackerel, and barracuda in Florida, albacore in California, salmon in Alaska, trout in many streams, and all sorts of other fishes, and the rod was the unstrained hero of a fight of over five hours with a Catalina yellowtail that got away.

That night the little Leonard took the brainiest fish of them all. On such a rod, with a six-thread line, the Grey Snapper as a game fish leaves little to be desired. And it was gorgeous fishing in the glorious tropic night along the clean white beach, with the sweeping beam of the revolving light increasing rather than lessening the sense of happy solitude.

The next day again I dug crabs; I did little but dig crabs. The method is simple—if you happen to know how. You repair to the beach. You find a hole at the mouth of which lies a little heap of sand. If it is dry you pass by on the other side. The owner is out. If it is moist, that is an indication that the owner has been busy housekeeping and is still at home. You thrust a long stem of beach grass to the bottom of the hole and let it, like your conscience, be your guide, as you dig with the tools nature gave you.

If you can find the crab before he is completely uncovered you may pick him up at your leisure, as placid and unresisting as a clam. But if he once starts to run, all you will see of him will be a swiftly diminishing perspective—all, that is, unless you have cunningly dug the hole so that he can not scale its crumbling sides. It takes brains to accumulate spirit crabs.

Still I got a whole lot of them, and only quit digging when the time came for the afternoon swim. That swim I shall never forget.

During that same morning a broad shouldered shark seven or eight feet long had come nosing along the shore past the Laboratory dock in three or four feet of water. I had tried to catch him, of course—it was no chance to miss—and I would have done it, too, except that the brute wouldn't take a cold Snapper just off the ice, which was all the bait I had. I knew, therefore, and by the most convincing proof, that sharks were around.

In the afternoon, and off the same dock, Doctor Mayer and I were swimming, he forty or fifty yards from the

[134]

Sea Tigers at the Dry Tortugas

beach, I well out beyond him. I chanced to glance down through the brilliant water, and there directly under me was a long black shape. Ye gods and great big fishes!

One glance was enough. I started for the shore at something over the average rate of a young spirit crab in the pink of condition, and as I reached Doctor Mayer I called out, "I think there's a shark out there."

"Is there? Let me look," was his highly unexpected reply, and he kept on swimming out. For the good of my soul I had to turn back and follow him, but I didn't like it—I didn't like it at all.

In a moment he reported, "No. It isn't a shark. It's only a log lying on the bottom."

As for me, I had nothing to say. I was too breathless to talk, for more reasons than one.

Such incredible fearlessness was altogether new to me. Respectfully but firmly, later on, I questioned him as to his philosophy on the subject.

"Well," said he, "I would rather have twenty years of swimming in tropical waters with the certainty of being eaten by a shark at the end than miss the swimming".

Naturally I asked him what made him think the shark would bridle his appetite for twenty years. But he waved that unparliamentary interrogation aside, and kept me silent with stories which made this much at least conspicuously clear, that I was more afraid of sharks than he was.

But to snap back to the Snappers. When we began fishing for them next evening they were ready for us—no end of them—except when now and then larger fish came hurrying up the coast—fish which in the dim light we took to be barracuda, but some of which, when we caught them, turned out to be sharks. Then the Snappers would disappear for a few moments. But they were soon back again.

After spirit crabs and the little Leonard had brought three or four Snappers to land, I cut up one of them as bait for the heavy rods we had brought along, cast out as far as I could get, and shoved the butts down into the sand so the rods could do their own fishing. Which they did, and in the course of the evening took four small sharks and a mutton fish of about fifteen pounds.

But that is not the point. The point is that within fifteen minutes after a piece of dead Grey Snapper in the form of bait had struck the water far outside of where we were fishing with crabs, not a single live Snapper was to be found where they had swarmed before. They seemed to be sunk without a trace.

By and by Mayer went back to bed, but I fished on in the moonlight, happy in the marvelous beauty of the tropic night, with the high blazing column of the lighthouse rising gigantic from the long low island set in the quiet sea. There were no more Snappers. I made up my mind that the tide must have turned and taken the fish with it. It was time to quit. But I had walked down the beach only a little way before the wise little Grey Snappers, more numerous than ever, were catching crabs ahead of me.

These self-educated fish knew that a walking man meant crabs; they knew that the neighborhood of dead Snappers cut into bait is no place for live ones; they were the same Snappers which for twenty days remembered that a blue hardhead was safe to swallow, but that when he is red it is unwise to drink him in. Luteanus griseus may have scales and a tail, but he knows more than many a man in pants.

Just Fishing Talk

SO THE Best Fisherwoman bought tickets to Long Key, because the Doctor said "take him South to get over his flu". And when we got there twenty-seven hours late (it had rained for nine days in flat and sandy Florida and the floods were abroad), it was the same heavenly spot as before, full of coconut palms and the smell of the sea, and inhabited exclusively by people who had forgotten everything in the world that was not fishing or concerning and appertaining to the same.

When Rubia judged I was strong enough she took me out to wet a line. Out over the reef we went to the deep clear blue of the Gulf Stream, where the sail-fish and amberjack and barracuda are, and all the rest of what Dr. Holder used to call "the delight makers", in ones and twos and schools and swarms, according to the weather and the whim of fisherman's luck.

One fish differeth from another fish in fighting method and power as well as in glory. The amberjack, to put it in that way, is a professional. Being hooked, he fights and does nothing else, wastes no effort, misapplies no pound of pull. He makes it just as hard for you as it can be made by a fish of his weight and inches. The sail-fish, on the other hand, has traces of the amateur. He plays a little to the gallery, flings himself out of his element, tears his passion to tatters, and exhausts no small part of his energy on the water and the air instead of applying it steadily and purposefully to the destruction of your tackle and the wearing out of the man behind it.

Rubia, who had hooked and brought, not to gaff but to a prompt release unhurt, seven amberjacks from twenty-five to forty pounds each, besides many minor fishes, in one day, had never taken a sail-fish, and I was keen to see her tame the wild cavortings of one of these picturesque and exuberant leapers.

I was calmly sure that it would be pie for her to handle a sail-fish if she got one on. That, however, was precisely what did not happen. Three strikes she had, two of which were obviously sail-fish, but with that perverse mischance which is merely the obverse of good luck, none of them were hooked. It was too bad.

Now I had taken sail-fish before, and being but a week out of bed, and shaky still, was perfectly willing to wait. So of course I had a strike and hooked whatever it was, and when nothing happened, announced that I had a grouper and prepared to pump him in—which, since I was fishing with a nine thread line, promised to be a long dull job. To pump I tried. There was no more response than if my line had been fast to a ring in the wall. Then a little yielding, more pumping, then more yielding, and within five minutes of the strike there came floating up to the boat on his side, without a fight, an unmistakable sail-fish, in what seemed to be very nearly a comatose state.

Still he was not comatose enough to allow himself to be hauled into the boat by his bill, and I had to give him line. Then more line. Then a great deal of line. And when he got that he began to jump here once, there twice, at first without much conviction about it, but apparently rather as a matter of form. Then more jumps, with more punch in them, more runs, and the line commenced to sing as it cut the water, and it began to look as if I had a real fight on my hands. And I had.

I was using a reel whose leather thumb brake was worn nearly through and limp with soaking, so that every now and then it would buckle under as the line came in, and that increased the interest. But the line (an old one), and the six ounce tip (a friend of nearly twenty years), were both perfect in their way, the boatman was cheerful and willing, the company was of the best, and every prospect pleasing except that man was vile—vilely soft and out of condition, and in no shape whatever to do justice to the situation.

My grandfather used to croon an old song to us children, the refrain of which was "the man ran and the dog ran, the man ran and the dog ran" repeated over and over again. Now it was "the man pumped and the fish ran, the man pumped and the fish jumped," until we had counted twenty-three jumps, and the multitude of runs, little and big, was beyond counting.

Pretty soon it began to feel like hard work, and every run meant so much more of it. Then it began to look serious, for every yard of line I lost meant a punishing effort to get it back. I started to hunt for reasons to believe that the runs were shorter and the fish weaker, but could not find any that were really convincing.

"Confound him, how long is he going to keep this up, anyhow?" Thereupon it became a personal matter between me and the fish. Protests arose within me over the perversity of this animate creature, and with that came the knowledge, slowly working to the surface of my mind, that either I was going to get him or he would surely get me.

By that time, in the words of another old song "my back was broke and my shoulder was lame." Then it was that the fish proceeded to go under the boat and go back under the boat, and hang under the boat until it seemed as if he had been born and raised there. Oh, I recognize that it was my own fault. I could just as well have kept the boat away from him till he was ready to be landed. I was giving the orders, and if he went under the boat no one was to blame but me. And the punishment did not miss me.

The sail-fish kept me plunging my rod into the water to the full stretch of my body and my arm, the boat having more than a plenty of freeboard, until once or twice the boatman just saved me, or thought he did, from going overboard altogether. Once I was slow in bending over and the line touched the sprag for an instant, but no harm was done and my breath came back again.

About that time I began to notice that I was having a hard time to keep my feet (it is my habit to fight a fish standing up), and to resent the way the boat was jumping about, which was neither more nor less than it had been doing all the afternoon. That was another trouble. Also my reel was an old fashioned one without a handle brake, such as too often I persist in fishing with, against all wise advice, and once it rapped my fingers good and hard, as such reels will.

Altogether it amounted to a considerable set of circumstances, with the fish still going strong. But the unkindest cut of all came from the Best Fisherwoman herself. One of the runs of the fish turned me so that I could see her sitting in the forward end of the cockpit. She wasn't agonizing over her sweat-drenched husband, fresh from his bed of pain, whose trembling fingers could hardly hold the rod or work the reel. She wasn't hanging upon the outcome of the struggle, hands clasped, lips parted, eyes astare. She should have been. As a matter of cold (even clammy) fact she was lost in a book, and not so much of a book at that.

When this vision burst upon my unbelieving sight, indignation possessed me and gave me strength, and since I couldn't proceed against Rubia with the physical violence which the situation plainly demanded, I threw every ounce I had left against the sail-fish, and took it out on him.

The sail-fish yielded. Closer he came at every circle, until at length we could see the glorious beauty of him plainly, and could see also that he was hooked in the bony cup which in the sword- and sail-fishes holds and protects the delicate fabric of the eye. Afterward I worked it out that the fish probably passed close to the boat, and must have been swimming toward and almost exactly in line with the approaching bait to have hooked himself just so. And of course the curiously mild beginning of the fight was thus explained. At the moment it meant only that he could not be returned to the water, and that the slightest touch upon the leader before gaffing might lose the fish.

When he came over the side of the boat one of the two hooks which the best sail-fish practice seems to require caught in the skipper's trouser leg. He asked me to cut it out. I did; but it took everything there was in me to get a knife out of my pocket, open a blade, and make the cut, so nearly powerless were my thumbs and fingers. No fish had ever so worn me out before, although this was no more than a fair sized specimen of six feet ten inches in length and forty-eight pounds weight. The landing of him should have taken from half to three-quarters of an hour. It did take an hour and a half, for which both the flu and the hooking in the side of his head may be held responsible. I am only sorry that the destruction of one eye made it impossible to let him go again.

With the fish in the boat, I was ready to go home—which was unimportant, because Rubia would have taken me in at once anyway, willing or not. So I went, and with me went sweet satisfaction and serene repose. The world was as it should be, the sea and sky beyond expression beautiful, hope beckoned, and I looked with cheerfulness upon the morrow. It had been a good day.

What is the master-feeling in sea fishing? "Boredom," says the Best Fisherwoman, looking up from her book, "and fear that the sun will ruin my complexion." But she knows that I know she is telling the thing that is not, for no one handles a salt water rod better or with keener satisfaction, or lands more fish.

"Hope realized that maketh the heart glad" says the man who loves to see fish in the boat. "Close contact with the wildest, freest, least known thing in nature," says the man who loves sea fishing, and not merely to catch fish. "A flooding sense of freedom and relief," says the man who left his job behind him, and I think this is the best answer of all.

Every man and woman of us that goes down to the sea in little ships to pursue our happiness in great waters has in common with all the others a host of small and great delights. We love the search for fish and the finding, the tense eagerness before the strike and the tenser excitement afterward; the long hard fight, searching the heart, testing the body and the soul; and the supreme moment when the glorious creature, fresh risen from the depths of the sea, floats to your hand and then, the hook removed, sinks with a gentle motion back from whence it came, to live and fight another day.

As it hath been said, and passing well said, "It is not all of fishing to catch fish." The hope of the catch, nevertheless, is the string upon which all the pearls of delight are strung. I love to catch fish as I love the fish when caught, and as I love to let them go. But to reach out into the illimitable ocean and take from it the gleaming creatures whose life haunts I can imagine but never really visit nor comprehend, and do it cleanly, honestly, with fitting tackle, my own ten fingers, and what understanding the Lord hath bestowed upon me—that is the extension of a man's personality almost beyond imagining.

Once we were anchored off San Clemente, in the cool brightness of a clear and vivid day. Beneath us we looked through the crystal water to where, sixty or seventy feet below, five or six pounds of yellowtail, an enormous bait, lay on the reef waiting for a strike. To it, out of the watery wings, entered the black sea bass, large, unhurried, and sedate. As we intently watched him he saw or smelled the great lump of fish, approached it, examined for some moments its surroundings, and then, setting his six or seven feet of length vertically above it, with his tail straight up and his head straight down, he sank upon the bait and with a single motion of his gills engulphed it.

I struck, he vanished in a cloud of sand, but the hook had failed to penetrate, the line fell slack, and I had lost him. What I can never lose is the unforgettable picture of the great fish feeding undisturbed a dozen fathoms down. What should I have gained if I had killed him?

Another time, we were anchored off the same shore in the early half-light of a breathless glassy morning. Fog lay over the water in a heavy blanket. The stillness made us speak in whispers. The world was listening, and every careless sound was an offense.

Suddenly out of the silence came the vast explosions of a blowing whale. Nearer they came and nearer, and then, so near a man could have tossed his hat upon him, up from the deep rose the form of Leviathan, grey, portentous, and immense, covered and then revealed by the cascading waters uplifted with him as he rose, and blew his terrific blast, and slowly sank again; and we all, awestruck and quiet, looked down upon the great flukes as they passed beneath our boat.

"Canst thou draw out Leviathan with an hook?"

Hm,—well, I don't know. What kind of a chance do you think a man would have with a 9/0 reel, three hundred yards of 36 thread line, and a Murphy rod? Anyway it couldn't hurt to try.

A Front Seat at a Whale

IT was one of those days that fill a man's heart with doxologies. To use an ancient simile, the air was like wine (if you happen still to remember what that formerly implied), the sea like the concentration of all beauty, and the fishing beyond praise. The tuna were abroad, strong as horses, swift as leopards, hungry as Gargantua himself. It was a poor day for a lazy man to be fishing.

To be at Block Island is to be twenty miles at sea, and every mile out from the Old Harbor adds to that number. It is small wonder that the fishing is of many kinds, and that what you do not go after is often what you get.

On that day of blameless intoxication (on less than half of one percent) the breeze died out toward noon, and although the tuna were still with us they were scarcer or less voracious, and it was time for lunch. As we sat fishing and eating, larger game than we were hunting swam into our ken. Quite near at hand, slow moving through a swarm of little fish, appeared Leviathan, and rose and moved and sank and rose again with the prodigious dignity that belongs to him alone.

Now whales have always had for me a curious attraction. Balaena or Balaenoptera, Physeter, Orca, or Delphinus, I love and long for them all. They fascinate me, whether by their size and power, or by the tremendous regions in which they pass their lives, or by their knowledge of the depths that man can never see, or perhaps by all of these together. I cannot tell you why, but I would rather see a whale than a movie; and how could I say more!

Beddard's *Book of Whales* has faced me across my desk
for years, and my copy of Andrews' *Whale Hunting with
Camera and Rifle* shows every evidence of hard reading.
How often have I seen in fancy the Antarctic beaches of
South Georgia piled with the skulls and bones of the fin-
back, greatest and swiftest of all whales? How familiar
is Hermann Melville's *Moby Dick,* whose involved and
mystical yet brilliant style has repelled full many a reader
from this incomparable classic of the sea. How often have
I read and re-read Frank Bullen's *Cruise of the Cachalot,*
and even W. H. G. Kingston's *Peter the Whaler,* and many
another story of the life and capture of the hugest creatures
that ever breathed the breath of life upon this mundane
sphere.

There is much to be known about whales. For instance,
not only do whales have hairs, but they are very particular
as to just how many they allow themselves. Thus it is
related of Balaenoptera borealis, in Mr. Beddard's book, that
the adult female has exactly twenty-six hairs on each side
of the lower jaw. Such meticulous exactness on the part
of a bearded lady is nothing less than extraordinary.

Although Mr. Beddard gives the size of adult whales
as "from barely four feet to as much as 80 or 85," others
are less restrained. He reminds us how Pliny, that Roman
naturalist who knew so many things that were not so,
asserted that "in the Indian sea the fish called balaena, or
whirlpool, is so long and broad as to take up more length
and breadth than two acres of land." Holland's translation
of Pliny makes it four acres. Either dimensions, seeing that
an acre is 208 feet square, may be regarded as ample.

Olaus Magnus was even more liberal. He allowed 960
feet in length to certain hairy whales, but since he divides
with Bishop Pentoppidan the well-earned glory of the

greatest sea serpent reporter in history, we may properly reduce his figures by 90 percent. As a matter of fact, the largest Rorquals, so far as my reading enables me to judge, probably reach 105 feet.

Much other valuable information occurs in Mr. Beddard's fascinating volume. Thus not only do we learn that one of the shallows-loving California gray whales is related by a well-known local authority to have run a whale boat's crew ashore and up a tree; but we are told also how in "Pontistes of the tertiaries of the Argentine the maxillary bones are more deeply excavated than in dolphins, and their posterior border is squarely marked off and extends farther back." Which might even justify that department store remark, "Ain't nature wonderful."

Volume I, part V, of the New Series of the Memoirs of the American Museum of Natural History, has long graced my bedroom. It contains the first of the monographs of the Pacific Cetacea, and deals with this same California gray whale, for twenty years believed to be extinct, but rediscovered by the author, Roy C. Andrews, in Korea in 1911. This is the same Andrews who has since become known the world around as the discoverer of dinosaur eggs. His paper not only confirms the hairiness of B. borealis from personal observation, but is otherwise very far from dull. To quote him (pp. 239 and 240) on a point much mooted among those who think of the sea as more than merely big and wet:

"The Gray Whales seem to be objects of continual persecution by the Killers (Orca orca); much more so than any of the other large whales. Among the first eight or nine Devilfish (the Japanese name for the Gray Whales) which I examined at Ulsan (Korea), three attracted my attention at once because the entire anterior part of the tongue had been torn away. Teeth marks plainly showed in the remaining portion and upon consulting the gunner, Captain Hans Hurum, who had killed them, he told me that it had been done by Killers at the time he shot the whales.

Seven Gray Whales were in the school, and shortly after he began to hunt them fifteen Killers appeared. The whales became terrified at once and he had no difficulty in killing three of the seven. When the Orcas gathered about, the whales turned belly up and lay motionless, with fins outspread, apparently paralyzed by fright. A Killer would put its snout against the closed lips of the Devilfish and endeavor to force the mouth open and its own head inside. This extraordinary method of attack was corroborated by Captain Johnson who had been hunting the same school of Gray Whales, and, moreover, by all the whalemen at the station who had witnessed it upon many other occasions.

"Out of the 35 Gray Whales which I examined especially, seven had the tongues eaten to a greater or less extent and one had several large semicircular bites in the left lower lip. The Killers do not confine their attention entirely to the tongue, for almost every whale which was brought in had the tips and posterior edges of the fins and flukes more or less torn; in several specimens fresh teeth marks were plainly visible where the fin had been 'shredded' as the whale drew it out of the Orca's mouth.

"Although none of the Gray Whales exhibited teeth marks on other parts of the body undoubtedly some of them are killed by the Orcas. A female Killer which was brought to the station had several pieces of flesh in its stomach besides a strip of whalebone three inches

The Flavor of Block Island

long. I could not positively identify the latter but believed it to have been from a small Devilfish. A male Killer was taken at the same time by Captain Hurum who told me that in the animal's death flurry it had thrown up two great chunks of flesh.

"Captain Melsom brought a Gray Whale to the station one day and I was interested to find the tongue almost gone. He said he had passed a school of Killers in the morning and later, after steaming about fifteen miles, had killed the Devilfish. A short time afterward, a long distance away, he saw the fins of a school of Killers which were coming at full speed straight for the ship. They circled about the vessel and one of them forced open the mouth of the dead whale to get at the tongue. When Captain Melsom fired at the Killer with his Krag rifle the animal lashed out with its flukes, smashing the ship's rail, and disappeared."

My passion for whales has nothing to do with Jonah, whom I regard as a deserter. Rather it dates from the time when, as a youngster just entering my teens, I saw the skeleton of a whale in the Old Museum at the Jardin des Plantes in Paris. Ever since then the Cetacea have gripped my imagination, and have never let it go. I recall with admiration—indeed with envy—the story of that Irish gentleman (in whose house I saw the harpoons he could not take with him when he died) who fitted out his own vessel and went to Greenland, as many another with less cause has gone to Africa, to hunt big game.

The Block Island whale that led to all this talk was not one of the giants. It seemed of moderate size, a humpback of 40 or 50 feet, but plenty big enough to be furiously interesting. We hastened to get closer, and I ran out to the pulpit on the end of the bowsprit as to a front seat in the balcony.

The whale moved slowly. As he rose, his skin glistened in the clear sunlight, a dark iron grey. As he sank again beneath the clear water, his color turned (suddenly and beyond all expectation) to a rather pale but distinct pea green. It was an amazing change, but plain and unmistakable. We followed the whale for perhaps a quarter of a mile, and saw the transformation in color several times repeated. It was unbelievable, but had to be believed. It was there.

But my attention was speedily distracted from scientific pursuits. In his enthusiasm for accurate observation, the skipper shifted his course, and from running parallel to the whale, and perhaps a hundred feet away, swung into his wake and came up behind.

Then I happened to look down, and saw directly beneath my feet the great flukes slowly churning the water into a boiling commotion as wide as our boat. If the whale had sounded at that moment he would have shot me into the air like a ball from a bat.

Nothing slower than a stop watch could have detected the minuteness of the time it took to review, and revise, and altogether readjust my opinions as to the desirability of a front seat, so to speak, at a whale. My mouth was opening to impart these sudden but deep-seated views to the skipper, when he threw over the tiller and we went away from there with speed. Not long after, the whale sounded, lifting his flukes majestically into the air as humpbacks do, and we saw no more of him. But the vision of how I might have appeared, winging my way up from the ocean into the blue, had he sounded a little earlier, continues to hold for me a certain melancholy charm.

Pickerel on a Plug

PLUG casting is a game I never really learned. It came into fashion after the days of my apprenticeship were over, and the current of my later fishing passed it by. The mysteries of thumbing the line or thumbing the spool were closed to me, and the stories of gigantic bass taken by casting after dark left me cold.

I was brought up to regard angling as the art of enticing a wary creature by the delicate presentation of its natural food, or what it must be induced to regard as such, and I thought scornful of all the tribe of plugs.

I was disposed to classify them with the other Jezebels and cover them all with an indiscriminate condemnation. I declined to offend the conscience of a fly fisherman by any dealings with the accursed thing. In this respect, at least, while I might not be happy, I proposed to be good.

But time brings changes. A dam broke, and trout with scarred sides began to fall to my Brother's rod and mine. The enemy was not merely at the gates, he was within them, and enthusiastically engaged in living off the garrison. The pickerel had got into our brook, and they had to be got out.

A pickerel spoon on the end of the sturdiest fly rod is clumsy and out of place. Live frogs, or any other form of live bait, are at least as much so. And anyhow I do not love to drive a hook into a frog or a minnow that can still feel.

At that time I had not learned the art and mystery of taking pickerel on a fly. Now for the first time in my life I was up against good fishing that I didn't know how to get.

Then from a forgotten corner of the mind revived what I had heard and read of plugs and the rods that cast them. Here was a possible way out. It could hurt nothing but my pocket book to try.

Rod, reel, line, plug came easy, but it appeared on trial that the art of casting did not. Trouble walked with me down this particular vale of tears. Every cast was a back lash, and every back lash a horrible mess. Nothing but my inheritance from a Puritan ancestry kept me at the job.

After a while some slight improvement began to dawn, but my best was still woefully bad. I hated myself for my clumsiness, I berated myself for my stupidity. I would have been glad to quit, but the wretched thing wouldn't let me alone. In my mind was the perfect cast I never got, close to my table stood the five foot casting rod, reel on, line threaded, and a casting weight on the end of it. The combination demanded to be used. So I dropped my work and used it.

After much practice progress became perceptible. At length back lashes were no more than one in half a dozen, and 50 or 60 feet of line followed the hookless plug with some regularity across the lawn. I was doing better.

To this stage setting of persistence and disappointment, enter the woman. Rubia, who has a habit of giving me the presents I am too niggardly, or too cautious, or too inert to give myself, presented me with one of the new fangled casting reels, which know as much as a good dog and are supposed to set the bungler on a par with the practised veteran. Of course they never do, but at least they help. This one reduced the back lashes to less than ten per cent, and suddenly I found myself not such a very unsuccessful caster. At that I opened a campaign against the pickerel.

Now like most men brought up on trout, the pickerel has for me a fascination I can not altogether understand. To catch a little pickerel in a pond compares but very feebly with taking at sea a fish of ten times his weight. Yet I question which provides the greater satisfaction. It must be, I think, a matter of my bringing up.

For his weight a pickerel is enormous; for his length he is reasonably game; and for his disposition he is a buccaneer, pirate, fresh water shark, and anything else you happen to consider vicious. There is nothing domestic about him, as there is about the catfish; nothing friendly, as with the sunfish; nothing gallant and debonair, as with the bass; nothing clean and fine and high, as with the trout.

Among the fishes of the Eastern Lakes and streams, the pickerel is the wicked partner. He is just plain bad, and he looks it. Moreover, he has all the fascination of his wickedness, a condition not absolutely unknown among scaleless vertebrates.

I know a fishing club far back in a desolate land, over populated with rattlesnakes, under-populated with humans, among the glories of which is the killing of a 90 pound lynx, and where pickerel grow big. Thither I took my new found interest in casting, and with it the reel that Rubia gave me, and the plug.

The plug was a sub-species of the innumerable genus wiggler, and it wiggled with amazing liveliness and success. I had been casting for less than half an hour when a tug that felt like a weed, but wasn't a weed, interrupted my reeling. Careful investigation disclosed a pickerel of 2½ pounds. I began to think better of plugs. And the best was yet to come.

Almost at the next cast after that one was landed came another tug—a long tug and a strong tug. Excitement filled me and the boat. So did anxiety. I just couldn't lose this fish. There ought to be a law against it.

Great Scott, what a swash! The rod bowed deeply to every shake of the savage head. It was the biggest pickerel I had ever seen.

When he came up, still fighting, and showed the deep lustrous green of his broad back, and threw himself viciously about, I was ready to swear to the virtue of every plug in every tackle shop in Boston—or I would have been if I'd had time to think about it. He was a whale.

Now to the sea fisherman, a whale, even a metaphorical whale, means a long hard fight—30 minutes to an hour, or two or three—yet here was the biggest pickerel of G. Pinchot's history, in perfect condition and fighting all he knew, yet unable to get a single inch of line, and netted, after several futile attempts, within three minutes of the strike.

As a fight, it was nothing—as an achievement it was immense, for my prize weighed 4 pounds 14 ounces, was 27 inches long, and headed the list of captures in that water for the past two years.

A five pound tarpon is a curiosity for its littleness, but a five pound pickerel is a wonder for its great size. Thus do we change our standards with our climate, and esteem the fish we take by how much more they weigh than those we are in the habit of taking. It's the old story of an inch on the end of your nose.

Porpoise Steak: part I

"YOU'LL be lucky if you get one shot in a year," said the Sage of Happy Valley.

"Time was made for slaves," said I.

"The porpoise is the wisest and the swiftest thing that swims in Florida waters," said he.

"Even the wise and swift may fall," said I.

"And in a canoe" said he.

"One can but try," said I.

"Try then, by all means," said he. "But when you do, take notice—"

And thereupon he laid before me the wisdom acquired in thirty summers of harpooning in the shoal waters of southern Florida; described how best the harpoon is to be made and thrown; told where, and when, and how, and why; and sent me on my way hopeful and rejoicing.

We were at Anthony Dimock's house at Peekamose in the Catskills, and I had been practicing, throwing a theorectical harpoon at a theoretical porpoise—a tin can off the stage—and not doing so badly, as I remember it, while Anthony looked on and gave me pointers. But about my getting an actual porpoise with an actual iron he had his doubts.

So had I. But I kept them to myself, and after I got home I went on practicing. I carried a hickory pole wherever I went, and whatever I saw I threw at. And every now and then I hit it.

From my youth up I had harbored a harpoon complex, but in highly unorthodox form. I always throw the har-

poon with one hand, like a javelin, as you have seen
Achilles do it in Chapman's Homer, Illustrated Edition,
and never with one hand to point and the other to propel,
according to the established ritual. Only I wear more
clothes.

Off the south shore of Long Island, when we were boys,
Carly Greene and I spent much time pitching a lily iron
out of a canoe at little sharks we seldom hit and never
got, for the lily iron is swordfish gear, and far too big
for such small game. And now Anthony had set me
afire again.

So the Milford blacksmith and I put our heads together,
and he made me three harpoons to Anthony's prescription:
A short shaft of half-inch round tool steel, a point less
than an inch in length beyond the barb, the barb out-
wardly knife-edged, to help it go in, but the angle where
it joins the shaft and inner edges carefully filed round to
prevent it from drawing out.

A fish on a hook pulls against the smooth curve of the
bend; the hook's barb merely keeps the point from slipping
out. But the barb on one of Anthony's tiny harpoons takes
the whole strain. Its edges must be round and smooth to
avoid cutting out through the skin of shark or porpoise
when the line pulls hard.

When the blacksmith had done his job (and he did it
well), I wound the shaft of each harpoon with rope, making a stop an inch back of the barb to keep it from going
in too far. Thus if the porpoise gets away there is no
serious wound to prevent his living to get away again
another day.

The socket which takes the harpoon pole must be short,
so that the pole can drop out easily when a fish is ironed.
The pole which fits in it should be long and light and

stiff. Cypress or pine will do, but spruce is the ideal wood.

But what is far more important than the pole is the harpoon line. Whalers use a laid manila rope, because they can find nothing else that is both light enough and strong enough. But more than one man has lost his life because the whale line kinked around arm, or leg, or even neck, and the diving whale took him along.

Harpooning such as I was honing for wants a line that cannot kink, and that means soft braided cotton. You can buy the sort I mean in balls. Just what its regular purpose is, I have forgotten. Certainly is has nothing to do with fishing.

This line is flat and no thicker than a pencil split in two. There's no such thing as a kink in it. And strong as you may be, even you can't break it with your hands. It will tow a canoe with two men in it behind the swiftest porpoise that swims. But before you undertake to play one on it be sure you have your glove. A whizzing line is sharp.

I had, as it happened, a commission to get porpoise skulls for a great museum of natural history. Also, I had an earned vacation due, and I proposed to spend it with the porpoises around Cape Sable. It was a grand combination and a happy thought.

Once before I had been in those waters, and had then succeeded, at the fourth attempt, after a most disgraceful exhibition of incompetence, in harpooning a fifteen foot two inch sawfish out of a skiff. Of course I was ashamed of that sawfish fiasco. Something had to be done about it. I went home and practiced some more, but without achieving any wonderful improvement. Harpooning, like many another art, to be well learned must be learned in youth. And there was Anthony and his porpoise prophecies. One shot a year. H'm.

So in due time the train disgorged G. Pinchot and his
outfit at Long Key. It was a morning in August twenty
years ago. And there was Tom Hand, one of the best
outdoor men I ever knew, and Colonel Lucius Watson with
his launch. Also there was my sixteen foot Otca Old
Town canoe, as good a model for rough water as ever I
had the luck to own. My fell purpose was to harpoon
porpoises out of that canoe. Tom was game; and we had
ten days to do it in.

Everybody in the North who heard of my intention was
scornful, to say the least. Everybody in the South jeered.
Take a porpoise in any such a peapod as that! Ridiculous!
Why not jump overboard at once and save yourself much
trouble? But Tom and I were set. We thought we knew
better.

We left Long Key in the launch one pleasant noon,
headed for the little frontier settlement of Flamingo, some
thirty miles away, where we hoped there was water fit to
drink, dry land enough to pitch a tent, and porpoises. We
towed our main reliance, the canoe, behind us.

Although midsummer, it was far from uncomfortably
warm. Sweet peace reigned over the Bay of Florida, which
spreads its shallows between the Keys we were leaving and
Cape Sable, long miles ahead. The water was clear, white
sand gleamed through it here and there, and the little
waves were flecked with brilliant blue. It all felt good.

Long slim needlefish—ballyhoo in the vernacular—
hustled over the surface before us, doing their specialty act
on their tails, which act consists of a rush out of water
and a gallop over it. Once above the surface they can
keep above it for fifteen or twenty feet, or sometimes a
good deal more, by working their tails furiously in the

A Sawfish Looks Like Nothing Else on Earth

water, after the manner and custom of flying fish and ballyhoos the world around.

As the launch chugged along we rigged a harpoon, flaked the line in careful zig-zags (not in a coil) in its flat wooden box, made it fast to the box (not to the canoe), set everything in order in the little Otca against the time of need, trolled for tarpon to pass the time, got nothing, lunched on crackers and alligator pears, and discussed our prospects. And missed the channel. If we hadn't missed it, we might have seen no porpoises that day.

About half past three the first pod of porpoises, to use a whaling term, hove in sight. We saw them raise their heads above the water while still a long way off, and look us over, and depart. That ended our chance of getting a shot at that particular lot.

The second pod we saw were in deeper water and busy with their fishing. Then there was arming in hot haste. Tom slipped silently out of the launch into the stern of the canoe, I into the bow, paddle in hand, the harpoon at my right, and the line in its box before me. It was a tense moment. One shot a year! Maybe this was it.

Tom and I worked the canoe as quietly as we knew how toward the little brothers of the whale. Not a paddle touched a gunwhale. Not a word passed. Fish can't hear. Porpoises can. These were fishing in a ring. We watched them make circle after circle, much under and little above the surface. This was a new and anxious game for both of us.

By good luck, and Tom's good sense, the canoe reached one edge of the circle just as every porpoise was at the other side. Now was the time. I stood up, ready, harpoon in one hand, line coiled in the other.

Tom swung the canoe head-on to a porpoise coming

straight toward us under water. Would he swerve or wouldn't he? He did. He didn't. He was coming fast. He was fifty feet off. Thirty. Twenty! I threw.

The harpoon struck, the pole checked, the surface exploded, the pole dropped loose, and the line leaped overboard. A hit and no mistake!

First chance. First shot. First hit. First fast fish. What would Anthony say to that?

In an instant the porpoise had snatched more than fifty yards of line out of its box. I caught the soft cotton in my gloved left hand, let it slip a little (I couldn't help it), and eased the canoe under way. And heaved a sigh that would have blown a full rigged ship a mile. This was what we came for.

The porpoise yanked us through the water at sizzling speed. Then he rolled over and over on the line and wrapped himself in it, like a shark, then rolled the other way. The next second he turned under the canoe, the next he spouted far off to one side, and the next was putting in his best licks fifty yards ahead of us. Suddenly the line went slack, and the first thing I knew I heard the fish (the porpoise isn't a fish, you know that) blow fifty yards behind us. He was travelling in the opposite direction hell-bent for election.

Tom worked like a maniac to swing the canoe, but no man on earth could have brought it about in time. My hands were full with the fish. Why not let George do it?

But if George jerked against me sideways to the canoe, he might turn us over. There was just one thing to do, and I did it in a hurry. I shifted the harpoon line so that it ran under the canoe. When the yank came, it would skitter us over the surface instead of snapping us upside down.

It worked. And before you could say Jack Robinson the porpoise had backed and twitched the canoe around, swapped end for end, and we were streaming out behind our motive power in the new direction, like a June bug on a thread. And right side up too, which is worth mentioning. He didn't get us that time.

But he might the next. In a moment he dove, and was off at high speed at a new angle. And then at another. And did it again and again till Tom and I had learned the game, and were letter perfect in our parts. We began to see that we could stand it as long as he could.

In spite of his swiftness in the straightaways, and his twists and turns and lightning changes, by using the porpoise to swing the canoe we kept close behind him. And the most line he got at any time was seventy-five yards. The light canoe had something to do with that.

Every minute or two our fish came up to blow. It was a harsh and alien sound, but somehow leisurely. And it was the only leisurely thing about him. The broad flat flukes were driving him and dragging us with a speed that made the water fly. Anthony was right about the swiftest thing in Florida waters.

Meantime the other porpoises stayed right loyally with their wounded brother. Their anxiety to help him was clear as a bell and very touching. No animals on land have ever equalled it in my experience.

But the fast fish was beyond their power to help. Gradually his rushes grew less dangerous, his breathing shorter, his runs less fierce. The harpoon, small as it was, striking just forward of the neck, or where a porpoise would have its neck if it had a neck, had done the business, and the end was in sight. But still there wasn't any time to stop and shake hands.

At length came the finish. The fight was over, and the game was ours. Three rousing cheers!

And not in a year, but in one day! Page Anthony Dimock. Whoops! We had the world by the tail with a downhill pull.

Now I concede that several things have happened in these United States that I never happened to hear about. But so far as I know this was the first porpoise ever harpooned and taken by an American sportsman out of a canoe, Indians and Esquimos excepted. If I'm wrong, and somebody beat me to it, I shall cheerfully yield the palm. But nobody can get away from me that first fight in the little Otca. That's mine for keeps.

And this first-day victory was no reflection on Anthony. He was thinking of skiffs. Hunting porpoises out of a canoe is altogether different. As it slides through the water, a canoe makes nothing like the fuss of a flat-bottomed skiff, and porpoises appear to regard its round green bottom as very much in their own class. Which is another score for my favorite fishing boat.

But how about throwing a harpoon while you stand up in your canoe? Well, in the first place, if you can't stand up, then stick to rod and reel. Harpooning sitting down would be like playing a piano with your toes. It has been done, but as a rule the best authorities don't recommend it.

In the next place, harpooning on your feet in a canoe isn't as ticklish as it sounds—provided, of course, the canoe and you are mates.

In Western stories written for Eastern tenderfeet, the horse and his rider are one and indivisible. When you see them in the movies burning up the ground on the trail of the villain who has abducted the beautiful maiden, the fact becomes self-evident. My personal experience with bucking horses, East and West, would indicate, however, that there are exceptions. No matter. You should be one with your canoe.

You balance it and keep it steady—it keeps you afloat. Its share in the operation of throwing the harpoon is just as large as yours. And you throw as freely as though you stood on solid ground. Unless you do, hunt no big game from a canoe, but get yourself a scow.

My Otca having lived up to everything I've said about it, the launch having come up, our problem was to get that first porpoise to Flamingo. We made his tail fast to the launch, and tried to tow him that way. He towed badly. Then we tried him the other way around. He towed worse. So we went back to the tail, and grinned and bore it.

But that wasn't all we had to bear by any means. The tide was going out, and the dark was coming in. We were caught on mud flats we couldn't cross, and we couldn't find the channel. So back we went to Sand Key, which we had passed a little while before, went ashore, hung our mosquito bars (cheese cloth, for a mangrove mosquito sails through mosquito netting like a bat through a window), and camped for the night.

We had no water, and we had no supper, and the mosquitoes were strictly as advertised. But what the night had in store for us was worth a dozen suppers and a thousand bites.

The arrangements were such that I missed nothing of it. I had a rubber bed. The rubber bed had a leak. And every thirty minutes it let me down on as fine a collection of cobble stones as you would care to see; whereby I was mercifully kept wakeful and attentive to the great show

[163]

the fish put on.

Our camp was on a narrow neck of land with the great stretches of the Bay of Florida on either side of it. The water all about us was crowded with great schools of mullet. Every instant, on one side or the other, or on both, some big fish would smash into these schools, hundreds of thousands of mullet would spring into the air in a wild effort to escape, and the roar as they tore out of water and broke in again was like the growl of all the lions in forty circuses, or the rumble of a heavy train over a trestle, or the thunder of a hundred drums.

I wish I could make you hear it as I heard it through the darkness of that interminable night—the long drum-roll of the mullet as they left the water, the crash of the big fish that drove them into the air, and then the louder roll again as the multitudes fell back. The intermittent sound of it was more like Niagara with the hiccups than anything else I can think of.

The thunder of one school of mullet had no sooner died away than the thunder of another began. Roar! Crash! Roar! For hours the diapason of life and death was almost continuous. It came from every direction, at every moment. How many millions of living creatures there were within reach of our ears that night, no man could tell. Nothing but astronomic distance seemed to offer a fit comparison.

It was a whale of a disturbance to be occasioned by fish only a foot or fifteen inches long. We knew the leaping fish were mullet, of course. The manner of their leaping told us that. But what their persecutors were we could only guess. Tarpon, or sharks, or porpoises, or all three, and others besides. Anyhow they were big and hungry, and on the job every minute till daylight did appear.

Meantime all through the night outside my bar the

mosquitoes sang their disappointed song. That was some consolation to a wakeful citizen, if I had needed any. There are times when a mosquito that can't get at you is almost better than no mosquito at all.

At dawn we had a swim in the shallow blood-warm water made roily by the multitude of fish. The sharks that bothered the mullet we gambled wouldn't bother us right up against the beach. They didn't, and we were off to Flamingo in the launch, canoe and porpoise towing behind us, both floating high—the porpoise a whole lot too high for human nourishment. The hot night had swelled him up like a poisoned pup, and the hot sun did nothing to help. So when we got to Flamingo we saved the skull and let the sea-beef go.

The highly self-reliant inhabitants of that diminutive settlement (just out of water and only just, with the Bay in front and vast swamps behind) we found to be of a ruddy and cheerful countenance, like David the King, instead of the sallow semi-invalids such surroundings would lead you to expect. There is no malaria at Flamingo. The mosquitoes in those parts are not licensed to carry germs.

At Flamingo we got first some water, then some breakfast, and then two important pieces of information. One was that there was an ice scow anchored a mile or so off shore for the accommodation of mullet fishermen who supplied the Miami market, and perhaps the man in charge would let us stay with him. The other item was why the Flamingoes, who sank their water cisterns in the earth, the tops level with the ground, kept a pole slanted between the bottom and the top of every one.

What was that pole for? For the snakes to climb out by, of course. You wouldn't want to let the poor snakes swim around in your drinking water till they died, would you? One big blacksnake that had fallen in was kind enough to demonstrate the value of this simple device while I was looking on. After which we filled our water can (at another cistern, but that was mere sentiment) and headed for the ice scow to ask leave from the man in charge to set up our tent on the top of it.

Porpoise Steak: part II

THE ice scow, anchored a mile off Flamingo, was a huge square-ended contraption with a flat-roofed house built on it. Early every morning the mullet fishermen brought their night's catch alongside the scow, put it aboard, and went home to sleep. So the man in charge, a big, gentle, lonely, and highly accommodating Swede by the name of Nelson, was hungry for company, and freely gave us the permission we were after.

We put up our tent on the aforesaid flat roof, braced it against the squalls that were sure to come, threw down our beds, dropped the mosquito curtain, and were comfortable. And safe against the buzzing stingers that flew out to us in swarms when the wind was from us to them. But when the wind blew off the shore, they couldn't scent us and stayed home.

To complete our housekeeping we anchored the launch just off the scow, hauled the canoe up inside the house, and moved our cooking kit into Nelson's kitchen. And there we were, snug as a bug in a rug, with no reason to envy the gaudiest blue-serge-white-shoe yachtsman in the grandest house-boat on this or any other water.

For many miles around the ice scow were the underwater mud flats of the Bay of Florida. Deep channels intersected the flats. These were the high road and hiding place of the porpoises. Out of them they came to their meals—meals on small fish on the shallows which were their table. We were right in the middle of our hunting ground.

But porpoises were by no means the only game in sight. The whole place was polluted with sharks. Like the porpoises, their feeding ground was on the flats, and there we went after them that same afternoon. But not in the canoe.

You can't harpoon sharks out of a canoe with even reasonable safety to the canoe, to say nothing of its crew and contents. On rod and reel, all the sharks you can hook you can kill with no risk to your cockle shell. So far as I remember, I've never seen a shark taken on rod and reel attack the boat, with two exceptions.

Once was off Block Island when I had warped a ten foot blue shark within gaffing distance, and Captain Harry Smith got a line around his tail. His business end was free to do business, and he left a considerable collection of perfectly good shark teeth in the counter of the launch.

The other time was when Rubia had brought one of her sharks-from-a-canoe alongside before he was sufficiently subdued. He was indignant and showed it, and the sound of his teeth tearing the canvas wasn't anything like Grieg's Slumber Song, and don't you think it.

A little thing like an iron in the back appears to disturb the serenity of many sharks, or even irritate them. When you go after these peevish pisces, I suggest a flat-bottomed skiff, and a solid one at that.

But doesn't it hurt a shark to break his teeth off on a boat? Not so you'd notice it. And if he smashes a few he has plenty more left. If you'll ask a shark to open his mouth and show you his teeth (and no doubt he will if you ask him politely), you'll find not one row, which is all you and I can boast, but maybe half a dozen.

You can't put a shark out of business just by extracting a few teeth, and if I were you I wouldn't try. Plenty more will come forward from behind to keep on making mince-meat at the old stand.

That first afternoon my diary says, "Struck two small sharks about five feet each and a stingaree. Missed on shot at a wake in the water. Otherwise 100% so far." Beginner's luck. Two days later the same veracious record records "Missed about 20 chances at sharks—was perfectly rotten." So fades the glory of the world.

Next day it blew. Everything being wrong for harpooning, I fell back on rod and reel. There were fish on ice in the ice scow, and the water dripping from them must carry their scent overboard. Therefore sharks must be nearby. That was sound reasoning, as the sharks proceeded to prove. Mullet they smelled and mullet they wanted. I wanted bites. We had no trouble in getting together.

I threw in from the scow. Bang! A shark was fast. As the line whizzed overboard, I jumped into the canoe, and that shark towed me all over the place while I put my back into it and fought my fish to his finish. Then it was back to the ice scow, reel in the shark, shoot him, cut out the hook, swell out my chest, rig a new bait, throw it in, and Bang! it was all to do over again. I had *such* a lovely time with those dear sharks!

The next day was Porpoise Day. We left the ice scow at six o'clock in the morning, towing the canoe behind a diminutive flat-bottomed power boat with an engine about the size of a can of beans. It drew about as much water as a tin plate. I hired it for that reason from one of the mullet fishermen. After an hour Tom picked up porpoises. There were four in that pod.

The first two saw us and left at high speed for parts unknown. The other two were fishing in a circle, as porpoises so often do. I suppose they corner a school of fish, so to speak, and the circling keeps the victims bunched till they can be eaten at leisure. Be that as it may, the two fishes paid us no attention as we paddled stealthily up in the canoe.

As with my first porpoise, the canoe waited on the edge of the circle. One of the two ran straight into us under water head on. It was a short shot and I threw hard. The iron struck just above the eye and crippled the fish badly. But when we came to look the porpoise over, it was a miracle that it could have fought at all, for the little harpoon had penetrated the brain.

Throughout the fight the larger porpoise, and several others that came up, hung anxiously around. To iron another would have been easy, but a poor return for fine devotion to a pal. They knew they were in danger and yet they stuck it out.

The fight lasted only ten minutes. Then the launch ran up with the skiff, and we hoisted our game into it. The harpoon had gone in clear to the stopping, but it came out easily, and the wound bled fast. The old ones left when they smelled blood. You couldn't blame them.

This porpoise turned out to be a calf only five feet six inches long, but at that he weighed a good deal more than I did. I certainly wouldn't have struck him if I had known how small he was.

Here was a beautiful animal (I mean just that, however little you might think it), with marvelous smoothness of skin and a clean and powerful outline, unbroken except by the high forehead, much higher than the forehead of a dog. The color was a light grey, turning to a rich coppery bronze a few hours after death. We took him back to our air-conditioned hotel, saved the skull, and put the tenderloins on ice.

We lived on those tenderloins, and their successors, all the time we stayed on Nelson's scow. And let me tell you, porpoise filet mignon is nothing to sneeze at. Sea beef is a little darker in color than land beef, but it hasn't the slightest flavor of oil or fish. It's good. I ought to know. I've eaten lots of it.

Later that day I got another chance, but a long one. A porpoise crossed the bow of the canoe and came within shot only when aft of the beam on the right-hand side. To throw at a fish in that position, when standing in a canoe, is a good deal like scratching the back of your neck with your elbow. And this one was a good thirty feet away besides. Did I get him? You tell. A miss is as good as a mile.

The following day not a porpoise. But up the channel, to the east of the ice scow, we began to find game. Tom with his marvelous eyes picked up a shark fin about as far as I could have seen the whole shark. Then it was boots and saddles. Which way is he pointed—How fast is he going—How can we head him off?

The shark was paddling along without a care in the world. Tom was putting everything he had on the pole. His job was to drive the skiff—the skiff, mind, not the canoe —to within twenty or thirty feet of that shark.

Now we were within fifty feet—now forty. At thirty I poised the harpoon. At twenty-five I threw. The iron struck just where the shark's fin cut the water.

He shot off over those shallow flats in a rush that was simply amazing. That shark drove his nose against the shallow water (it must have been only a foot or so deep) so hard that, having no place else to go, it had to rise in a sort of rainbow over his back. It sounds like pure invention, but I saw the same thing many times on this trip.

Tom picked up the harpoon pole as the shark yanked us past it. We skimmed over the water behind him for at least a quarter of a mile. Then he got over his panic and stopped to fight. He threshed about all over the place, throwing water in all directions. We began to creep up.

As I pulled the skiff cautiously closer, I could see that he had the chain that connected the harpoon and the braided cotton line clamped hard between his jaws. He was trying to cut it but having poor luck.

Tom handed me the .45. But before I could shoot the shark charged the boat and struck it with a great jolt at the angle where side and bottom met. I could hear the crunch as his teeth drove into the wood.

I saw him coming and was ready when he hit, crouched down, with a firm grip inside the boat. His head was in reach of my hand as he ground in his teeth and jerked at the boat like a dog fighting a rope. Then the Colt came into action, the powder blast threw water all over us, the ball found the brain, and that shark was permanently reformed.

This particular marauder being disposed of, the hook cut out, the chain pried loose and wound around the pole again, and the line made fast with a jam knot at the end, we were ready for the next.

Then across the flats came in sight another shark. Tom worked his head off to get me up to him. And all I did was to miss a perfect shot. Off went my target with the rush that thrills, and it was small consolation that the next throw hit the mark.

The mark was a seven-foot fish like the first one. The iron struck him in the brain and stopped him dead. That one left no teeth in my skiff and never would.

The next one never stopped to fight, but ran and ran till I pulled the boat up to him and gave him his quietus. He was an unworthy son of a fighting race.

That day I struck seven sharks and got five, from five and a half to seven feet. The other two got away.

Also I struck a tarpon that made a superb rush and towed the skiff 500 yards. That tarpon put up a fight that would have done honor to a shark of twice his eighty pounds. When it was over I turned him loose. He'd earned it, and the little harpoon had done him little harm.

Eight fish ironed and five sharks shot in one day sounds like good work. Well, that was the day I missed the twenty sharks.

And as to shooting sharks, it's no manner of use to perforate one of these lowbrows through the body. A shot outside the three places where you can really get results hardly does more than arouse his curiosity. But if you shoot him in the nose, which is the seat of a smelling apparatus that would put a dozen bird dogs to shame, or through the brain, which in a 7-foot shark is smaller than the first joint of your thumb, or through the gills, with which he does his breathing—then he's your shark.

But do I mean to tell you that a shark has a better nose than a bird dog?

I sure do. Perpend:

A shark must have a nose, for he makes his living by it. His meat is crippled fish and dead fish. His nose has to find them for him. I've seen many a shark swim close by healthy fish and pay them no more attention than they paid to him. But hook one of these indifferent spectators and let him show that he's in trouble, and Old Man Shark will be on the job in a split second.

Next time you catch a shark, get out your snickersnee

and go inside. In his head you will find a smelling apparatus at least ten times bigger than his brain, with the most elaborate provision for extracting every bit of scent there is in the water—the water that gets in through a slit on each side of his head and circulates around what look like a finer set of gills.

A shark's nose is built to deliver the goods. For example:

One day we were chasing in the launch a big shark we never got. A small shark crossed our course. I threw and missed. The small one ran hard and straight, and kept on running. That incident seemed closed.

But another and a bigger shark, swimming along with nothing to do and plenty of time to do it in, ran at right angles into the scared one's trail, after the scared one had gone by at least a hundred yards. The instant the strolling shark struck the trail of the shark I had thrown at, it whirled violently about and rushed at full speed along its own back trail.

There was nothing to account for it but the scared one's trail. Evidently the frightened fish had left a scent behind it that upset the shark that had not been thrown at till he was as nervous as the shark that had. Thanks to their noses, among sharks fear is catching a long way off. My diary says: "This shows why so few sharks are about this day—we have run them out. I missed only three sizable sharks all day. They were scarce."

Just to show you how scarce they were, here's the diary's tally for that day of dearth and deprivation:

"One shark, six feet ten. Struck him square in middle of the back with one of the fancy double toggle irons the tackle shops work off on the unwary, and it instantly pulled out. A hard blow—so hard it partly stunned the fish. Got him later. (That was duck soup. He was not himself.)

"One shark, six feet four. Missed easy shot as he came directly toward us, then struck him on long straightaway shot. (Having been little hunted, they often gave me a second chance.)

"One shark, five feet—a long straightaway shot through top of fin. This shark made a superb run and kept on running. Made no rolling fight. (That was when they bit the chain and rolled the line around them.)

"One shark, five feet eight. Struck as he crossed us at not less than 30 feet. (Every now and then I did make a decent shot.)

"One shark, six feet. This one I missed once and then after a long chase struck him from the bow of the launch." (Poor work, but I got him.)

That whole country was just crammed with sharks. A scarcity of sharks there would have been plenty anywhere else. The mullet fishermen were so bothered by these buccaneers that we stood ace high with them because we were doing what we could to reduce their numbers.

At the end of their first rush most of those I ironed turned to fight. They were no sand sharks but just chock full of sand.

Practically all the thirty odd sharks I took tried to cut the line. They had the chain gripped between their teeth when we got up to them. One had it round his head and through his mouth twice. Sharks' teeth polished that brass chain till it shone like gold.

When the skiff was near enough to see what the shark was doing with the chain, it was usually near enough for him to charge—and that charge was no slap on the wrist. Over half of the sharks harpooned on this trip hit the boat, and when they hit it they hit it hard.

The biggest shark of all, a heavy brute, charged the boat so suddenly and so viciously that he almost knocked it clean out from under me. Before I could crouch down I was upset. Luckily I fell in the boat and not in the water. It was just as well.

That shark's jaws were a good foot across. When we came to cut them out we found his face full of the stingers of stingarees, slim ivory daggers four or five or six inches long, saw-edged like a poisoned arrow, and covered with a black skin which to a human is just about as poisonous.

This skate-like fish usually carries several of these most unpleasant weapons near the root of its tail. I never heard that a man ever died from the wound of a stingaree, but when a man is struck, he's going to be sick, and for more than a day or a week. But this gentle and sensitive member of the Squalidae lived on stingarees, and their stingers made no never-mind in his young life.

The moral of all this is plain: Like cornered rats, sharks are tough babies if they can't get away. When your canoe takes you harpooning, stick to the porpoises and let the sharks alone.

I wish you could have been with us through one day's routine. Up in the dawn, cool and delicious, as the sun began to color the smooth waters of the Bay, and smoke arose above the little cluster of houses at Flamingo in the distance. Then a bath with a bucket. No swimming off that scow—not on your life.

And after that, breakfast in Nelson's cuddy on porpoise tenderloin and what have you, a breakfast that just exactly filled the bill as we planned our day's campaign. And then the hunt.

Off we went in the launch, Watson at the wheel, Tom

on watch, and G. P. drinking in the beauty of sea and sky and atmosphere, and very keen for action. And as we went the life of the great flats was opened before us—the whip rays and the sting rays, the redfish and the tarpon, and many a conch and hermit crab, and many a cloud of mud that concealed we knew not what, as something got away. All the vivid living of the hunters and the hunted in that happy hunting ground was part of our lives too, through the long day, and until the serenity of evening brought us back to another meal of porpoise steak.

Porpoise Steak: part III

ON ONE gloriously beautiful day we were out to collect a Bay of Florida porpoise—August 26 it was, to me a day well worth remembering. Tom paddled me up to a group of three. We caught up as they found a narrow channel, and they were out of sight in it as we passed over them. They saw us, they rushed, and the tail of one of them hit the canoe. It seemed to mark a sort of intimacy with porpoises.

But that is by the way. What set the day apart came after we sighted and followed four others. They played about us just out of reach, and then left us and joined six or eight more that were fishing in very shallow water. We reached the neighborhood of that pod, worked our way closer, got almost close enough.

With harpoon in hand and the regulation ants crawling up my back, I stood up. The porpoises bunched and started off. But one big old fellow, with a notched back fin, got separated from the rest and couldn't stand it. He had to get together with his crowd, and he crossed our bow to do it.

I threw at twenty feet. The iron struck him above the right flipper. He rushed. The others all rushed with him, and that rush made our canoe feel mighty small.

This was a wise old bird. He snatched the canoe through the water at dazzling speed, like a match in a mill-race, then rested without coming up. I pulled the canoe up to him, he rose once very near us, with a great Whoosh!, went down again, swerved under water, and made another fierce rush square at right angles to the way he was headed when I saw him last. He whisked that canoe about as if it were a child's toy boat.

Next time, his broad flukes drove him under the canoe, and he made his mighty rush straight off behind us. We just did get her round. Then he changed direction, under water and out of sight, in the middle of a run. And every run was like wildfire. Tom and I had all we could do, and a little more, to keep the Otca following him on an even keel.

He was hard hit, but there seemed no end to his vitality and power. The iron had gone deep, and the bloody spout told us it had touched his lung. But that soon stopped and it never weakened him.

Rush, blow, set the waves circling, rush off again. Tom swung the canoe this way and that with every ounce he had, I set the line across her bottom, the porpoise skittered us over the surface as if we didn't weigh a pound. We just did manage to keep her right side up in spite of him.

This hectic struggle went on for an hour, and then for another, and then for still another. My arms ached, my eyes were full of sweat. Could we never wear him out? It seemed so. If this kept up much longer the harpoon would wear its hold thin and then pull out. We had to kill him or lose him.

I drew the canoe up close, only just beyond reach of his beating flukes, and shot him in the head with the .45. He gave one great surge. Beyond that, no more effect than if I'd shot a wave.

Again the same cautious approach, same shot in the head, same result. And again. Every ball hit, but he seemed invulnerable.

One of the shots did seem to slow him up, but he got

over it in a minute. At the end of the third hour he was going strong. That was the first time I ever met anything that wouldn't take notice of a .45. There was nothing left but to lance him.

The lance was under the thwarts. Tom got it out. I pulled up close again, Tom swung the stern around to keep us from the flukes. With the line in one hand and the lance in the other I went into action.

The first thrust missed. Too much excitement. The porpoise kept right on. The second hit him. Up went his great flukes and down in a blow that would have squashed us if we'd been under them. We weren't. Tom saw to that.

The third thrust pierced the lungs and found the life. Instantly he threw himself on top—beat the water into foam—rushed across the surface in a ring—blood pouring from his blow hole. How long it went on I was too excited to note. It was tremendous.

This was the circular flurry that all whaling stories tell about. He would have knocked us galley west if he had hit us. The waves of his agony rocked the canoe like surf.

Then the flurry ended and the great beast sank. Big bubbles came to the top before he died. We sat and watched them burst. And caught our breath. Whew!

Our porpoise lay on the bottom, like a sunken wreck. We had to raise him by the harpoon line. Would that tiny iron pull out or would it hold? It held; the rounded edges refused to cut the skin; the launch came up; we made him fast. He was ours for keeps. We felt like millions of dollars. And then some!

Now we could take our time. Deliberately we towed victor and vanquished, canoe and porpoise, to the ice boat, and hauled our prize out to measure him. His length was eight feet four inches; his girth, five feet eight inches. He was a broth of a boy.

We couldn't weigh him, for we had no big-enough scales. But if the tarpon formula holds for porpoises—the square of the girth in inches, multiplied by the length in inches, divided by 800—then this porpoise's fighting weight was 578 pounds. Which probably was away below the fact, for a porpoise is a lot solider and therefore must be heavier than any tarpon, measure for measure.

Or put it this way: This porpoise was more than half as long as the canoe and he weighed at least one hundred pounds (or more probably upwards of two hundred) over and above Tom and me and the canoe, with our harpooning equipment and everything else in it, all put together.

He was an old male and an old warrior, scarred all over with the marks of battle. His dorsal fin was nicked at the end, and a strip had been bitten out of its rearward edge. His flukes were badly lacerated. The other scars were mostly between the dorsal and the small. And if you don't know which is the small, why, it's the sort of isthmus where the flukes join the body. Read the description of the whale in *Moby Dick*.

The marks upon this ancient scrapper, from their spacing, apparently were made by porpoise teeth. (I've seen other porpoises scarred in the same way.) His own teeth were slightly worn, as befitted his obvious age. In size and shape they were much like the fangs of a grey wolf.

Some of the heavy bullets fired at this veteran were stopped by his skin and the outer layer of blubber, and hardly got into his flesh at all. Not one of them penetrated far enough to crack his skull, to say nothing of getting inside it. We would probably have done better to use a seventy-five.

Nelson put by some of the oil from the fat about his

forehead. I understand that's what they use for lubricating watches. We hung his tenderloins over a cake of ice in the big cold room of the scow. His beef was very good in flavor, but a little tough, which was not surprising.

We saved his cranium, of course. The rest of him we delivered to the sharks, as some slight acknowledgment of their contribution to our entertainment. Porpoise meat is a shark's ice cream. He'd rather have it than a halo, any day of the week.

Cleaning a skull, for one who is no expert, is a messy operation. I know how to sluice out the brain with a stick and a little water through the hole the spinal cord goes through. But that is just the opening number. When I came to put the final touches on the three porpoise skulls we had amassed, it occurred to me that the crabs and the sand fleas would do a better job than I could. So I strung the three of them on a piece of rope, paddled ashore, and tied them to a stake in water about a foot or two deep at high tide.

And when I came back to check up on the sand fleas, the skulls were gone. And the museum was shy three crania. Perhaps it would have been different if I had gone to the ant instead of to the flea, which, not being a sluggard, I did not do. The skulls might have been safer on shore. What carried them off in the water I can only guess. At the time I thought it was a shark. I am not so sure today. It could have been a Flamingo.

Not all our days were filled with porpoises of heroic size. Once we went over to East Cape Sable, the nearest of the three capes that make one cape on the map, to have a look at the thousands of coconut palms some one had planted for miles along the shore. It was pleasant to rest my sunburn in the shade, and listen to the rustle of the long fronds

Tom Hand Gaffs a Good Little Shark

in the breeze.

There was a crumbling dock, a pretentious club house, or so the Flamingoes called it, deserted and decaying, a tank of bad water (perhaps they forgot the snake pole), and a very few mosquitoes. Also there was a cheerful old citizen, the sole inhabitant, living in a little cabin of rough boards, most beautifully tinted inside.

Tinted by what? By mosquitoes, indirectly. The smoke of its smudges hung round it still, and gave its walls the most exquisite brown shade you ever saw.

We shared our lunch with the old boy, who showed me how to blow a conch shell, told us he had a brother buried there (reason not given), and generally made Tom and me at home. I imbibed two drinking coconuts and wished I hadn't. Two was one too many. And altogether I was glad I came.

The place was simply swarming with fish. Many small tarpon were feeding just off the dock. I caught one and turned him loose, then took a mackerel shark and a shovel-nose on heavy tackle. That was in my regular line of business. So being inordinately puffed up, I tried a nine thread line on a fly rod, for novelty and foolishness, and promptly lost the whole of it to a fish I never saw.

And then, forced back to heavy tackle, I got hold of a stingaree, and there was the deuce to pay. It flew up and down and all around the town in spite of the best I could do to prevent it.

Finally the stingaree settled on the bottom, in a way these flat-fish have, and the heavy rod and twenty-four-thread line were powerless to pry him loose. The fishermen say suction is what does it. Certainly it isn't weight, for with such tackle I've often lifted fish that weighed six or eight or perhaps ten times as much as this one.

Anyhow I couldn't do a thing with this particular corn plaster. We had to take the skiff and follow the line down with the lance through the shallow water before our shark's-meal would listen to reason. Then we found he was only three and a half feet across the wings, and had but a single sting.

After which, Home, James, to the Ice Palace! As the sun got ready to set behind the palms, and smoke unused for decorative purposes rose from the old conchblower's cabin, Tom and I called it a day, and a good one.

The day before our time was up we got to windward of porpoises in another pod of four and let the southerly breeze blow us down to them. One of them crossed our bows at thirty feet or over, under water but dimly visible. I struck him at the junction of flipper and body with the stopped iron. He rushed, then cast himself clear of the water in one superb perpendicular leap, turning in evident amazement to look at us, and shaking himself against the sting of the harpoon. He was as big as our biggest.

At precisely the same instant, two others of the same size made the same leap. They made it in perfect time with the fast fish, to the same height, at the same angle, and their eyes, like his, were on us as they rose.

The three fish were hardly a biscuit toss away. It was a gorgeous sight. The waves of the first jump had not reached us when the fast fish jumped high in the air again. Both times I saw the harpoon sticking in his side. Then it pulled out. With that, our hunting ended.

This porpoise was hit hard. It was clearly the rope around the harpoon shank, the stopping, that lost him. All right, suppose it was. The stopping is a fair and decent way to give your game his chance. Moreover, the sight of these three comrades, shot out of their element to hang an

[184]

instant in the air, to me was worth at least as much as to kill one of them.

In my ten days I got seven shots at porpoises; missed two, one at thirty feet, and one at forty; struck two that got away; and took three. At the rate of seven shots in ten days, Anthony's year would have produced 252 shots and 108 porpoises—it would, that is to say, if I had been willing to kill them, if they had been willing to let me, and if the supply of porpoises had held out.

Porpoises have personality. A porpoise isn't just a lump of blubber out in the wet. I came to the conclusion on this trip that a porpoise knows as much as a bear, and that's a lot. The more you see of them the more you'll think so. There's a lot more in a porpoise than meets the casual eye.

Did you ever hear of Pelorus Jack, a porpoise that for years used to meet steamers at a certain place in Torres Straits and travel with them for an hour or so just to be sociable? Or have you seen these swift and playful companions of the waves crowding about the bow of your ship and keeping pace with it, as a dog tries to keep up with a motor?

We found it almost useless to follow any porpoise that had once taken a good look at us. More than once we saw them raise themselves in the water, examine us with one eye, then turn and examine us with the other, obviously disapprove of us, and then make off. If they had spoken out they could not have been more definite in their opinion.

Porpoises look clumsy, of course. Their figures do not conform to Paris fashions, and neither do they alter with the same. Having no waist, they cannot shift it. But they do make an impression of real cleverness when they size you up with their intelligent dark eyes.

And they can see more than a rod or two with those

melting glances, which may not seem as sentimental as a camel's or as cunning as an elephant's, but certainly have brains behind them. One porpoise looked us over and ran when we were all of 150 yards away. Like enough we had already chased that one. Another time a pair of them seemed to take our measure from under water, for they turned sharp at thirty yards and beat it without coming up.

But that is nothing. Listen to this. You may find it harder to swallow than a mullet is to a porpoise. Nevertheless it did happen, and out under the brilliant midsummer and midday sun of the Bay of Florida at that. Take it or leave it, this was it:

One day near Porpoise Point we found a school of porpoises—four fish fishing. It was fishing straight out of Alice in Wonderland. These porpoises "welcomed little fishes in with gently smiling jaws" by a method that hardly could happen outside of a fairy book.

I myself saw, and saw distinctly, one of the larger porpoises of this pod throw little fish into the air with his tail and catch them in his mouth before they hit the water. This fellow lay over almost on his back, from one-third to one-half of the whole animal out of water, and kept striking toward his head with the other end of him, as you might flap the fingers of your hand against the heel of it. Small fish were flung toward his head, or perhaps jumped to get away from the flailing flukes, and he snapped and snapped at them as they fell.

The tail churning up the water, the little fish gleaming in the air (mullet I thought they were), and the open jaws catching at them as they fell were in plain sight, and I, G. Pinchot, saw them. To me it was an amazing sight. I judge it would have been to you as well. It made me bat my eyes, but it was nothing new to Tom or Watson.

Now what do you think of the intelligence of porpoises? A trained seal couldn't beat that.

This porpoise saw us but did not let that worry him. He merely kept out of harpoon range, and I confess I wasn't sorry.

And here's another story you won't believe without some trouble. One perfect day we picked up some porpoises over a mile away by the spray they threw up in their fishing, and went after them. Tom and I in the canoe got between two of them. They saw us, but with the usual porpoise willingness to take any chance to get together, in a rush to join the other one of the two passed us about thirty feet away.

Thirty feet is a long harpoon shot from the water's level. Still I threw. The pole went true, but the line went slack. I thought I must have missed.

But when I came to look at the harpoon, the thin point, which a moment before was in perfect condition, had been bent over in a complete half-circle. Instead of pointing forward it was pointing backward. I couldn't believe my eyes. But Tom saw what I saw, and so did Watson. And both of them had heard the iron strike.

I couldn't believe it, but there it was. I couldn't lay it to a stone. There are no stones in that soft mud. I couldn't lay it to a shell. If the point had hit anything hard enough to bend it, it would have been badly bruised. There wasn't a scratch on it anywhere. Gee, what hides these porpoises must have!

And yet how could the armor of a crocodile, let alone the skin of a porpoise, stand up against the blow of that tool steel point, sharp as a needle, and with the weight of a long pole and the full power of a six foot man behind it? But there was the bent point in my hand. I gave it up.

Years afterward I got the answer. Talking to an old

whaleman at New Bedford, it occurred to me to tell him this true tale and ask him what about it.

"Of course," said he, "every harpooner knows that an iron'll bounce back from the skin of a whale if the fish's body is bent (he meant concave) toward the harpooner, and the iron strikes where the blubber is slack."

There is it. Believe it or not. In either case I have told you all I know about it.

This story deals with sharks and porpoises, but I wouldn't like to have you get them mixed. Every once in a while you'll see a porpoise in the movies shown for a shark, or vice versa, but there's nothing criminal in that. Still the differences between sharks and porpoises are by no means confined to the way they behave about biting canoes:

A porpoise is a mammal; sharks are fish. A porpoise has warm blood; sharks cold. A porpoise breathes air; sharks breathe water. A porpoise has flukes that lie flat, like a whale's; sharks have tails that stand up and down as fish tails do. A porpoise has bones, and very solid bones at that; sharks have no bones at all, but only gristle.

A porpoise has round white teeth like a dog or a bear; sharks have all kinds of teeth except that kind—and most of them are sharp as the edge of old Tobin's jackknife. A shark may use them on you, but a porpoise won't.

A porpoise has a dark and liquid eye. A shark's eye is a slit out of which looks wickedness—exactly the same slit you can see in any rattlesnake, and not a bit more Hollywood—an eye to fit a cold-blooded, selfish, stupid perambulating appetite.

Hit him again, he ain't got no friends! That's the way pretty much everybody feels about a shark. I do, and I'll bet you do. Most folks—even the most refined—love to read about shark massacres.

Every sailor hates a shark, and some of the things sailors do to sharks are anything but pretty. Greek and Roman mythologies, on the other hand, are full of tales of ship-wrecked sailors carried to safety on the backs of porpoises (dolphins, they used to call them, but a dolphin of today is not a mammal—it's a fish). And modern sailors have a fellow feeling for them, however seldom they may act as life-boats in these degenerate times.

I have a fellow feeling for them myself. Why not? A porpoise is a highly intelligent animal, generously eager to help its friends in trouble, and devoted to its young. I have seen a porpoise mother refuse to be driven from her calf by the most imminent threat of death.

But I went porpoise hunting? Yes, I did. I had a perfect scientific reason, just as T. R. did when he went hunting beasts in Africa. Museum specimens is what we both were after. Just so we took a few for specimens from the schooner *Mary Pinchot* on her voyage to the South Seas, because the National Museum asked us.

But since I got to know about them all the things that I've been telling you, I've gone no more a'hunting for these lov-able and interesting fellow creatures, and I don't expect to.

Lovable? Sure. I wouldn't care to hold one on my lap, but if all the qualities I've told you about don't make a person or a porpoise lovable, then magnanimity is dead upon the earth, my doll is stuffed with sawdust, and I want to be a nun.

I love a canoe as much as ever, and my eye and arm seem to be little the worse for the years. But hereafter any porpoise can parade his sea beef across the bow of my canoe in perfect safety. He's free of the seas for all of me.

Tree Climbing Angle
Worms

TO US on the schooner *Mary Pinchot* who were so happy
as to see it, Hanavave, on the island of Fatu Hiva,
Marquesas Archipelago, French Oceania, is nothing less
than the most beautiful spot in the world.

Indeed, most of the Marquesas Islands are far beyond all
common experience—at least beyond all my experience—in
picturesqueness pushed to its uttermost limit. They are
gorgeous and theatrical. They bring irresistibly to mind the
most imaginative efforts of the least restrained scene painters.
They are beautiful with a vividness and extravagance and
unexpectedness of form and color which leave one entirely
without adequate comparisons. In the old cant phrase, they
must be seen to be appreciated.

Centuries ago Spanish explorers sailed into a bay on the
west side of Fatu Hiva. They called it the Bay of Virgins,
not for an earthly but for a Heavenly reason. They gave
the bay its name not because of the swarms of young girls
who doubtless swam out to welcome them (Marquesan
women of those days had to swim because it was death
for a woman to touch a canoe), but because huge rounded
pinnacles of volcanic rock about its shores looked to them
like cloaked and hooded figures of the Virgin Mary en-
shrined for worship.

These tremendous natural simulacra are many. They are
scattered on the margin of the bay and in still more colossal

magnitudes for half a mile beyond. They dominate the nearer scene, and they look the part their name assigns them.

It takes but an instant of time and the minimum of good will to see these titanic figures as Virgins still today. But day after day must pass before custom can begin to dull the wonder of the place and make its beauty and its unreality realized and real.

I can no more make you grasp the Bay of Virgins with mere words than I can adequately describe diving among the living corals and gorgeous fishes of Tuamotuan lagoons. Not Stevenson himself, master of language, could make the Marquesas vivid in his pages. How, then, could a casual like me?

The Bay of Virgins (or of Hanavave) is a little bay. It is far narrower than the height of the hills which rise straight up from the water's edge. It is as strange as it is beautiful. The whole scale and contour of the place are so exceptional that when we had dropped anchor well within the headlands in eleven fathoms and I asked our Captain how far we were from the shore that seemed within a biscuit's toss on either side, he frankly said he couldn't tell, but would take the launch later and find out.

At the head of the little bay lies a steep and difficult beach of black lava boulders against which the long Pacific roll breaks in a surf heavy enough to require care in landing, and back of that the little village of Hanavave, set, like other Marquesan villages, in its groves of cocoanuts. Like many another it fills the constricted mouth of a great valley on whose produce the people live.

They are simple, kindly, honest, and most hospitable, these Marquesan people, who have lost their old life, their old habits, amusements, customs, many of which were worthy to be preserved. Before the pressure of a more vigorous race they have yielded most of what they had, and except for the one great blessing of Christianity, they have been given little enough to take its place. Civilization has given them disease, and clothes, and kerosene, and canned goods, and in return has taken away their ancient joy of life.

At present the Marquesan people are perishing—victims, first of all, of white men's sicknesses; then of white men's domination, which has destroyed their pride of race; and, finally, of the loss of interest in a life that has become flat, stale, and unprofitable. Quite literally, they are bored to death and dying of it.

At this village and at Omoa, four miles away, with not over 150 people all told between them, our surgeon, Doctor Mathewson, made forty visits in the five days of our stay. There was work enough to keep him busy for a month, could we have remained, before even the most obvious and pressing medical needs could be met. But that is another story.

We established our position with the natives of Hanavave with precision and dispatch. The anchor was hardly down before we brought ashore two pigs that had come with us as passengers from Hiva Oa, for which we had been charged 45 cents a pound on the hoof by the Compagnie Navale et Commerciale de L'Oceanie—the most expensive pigs, so far as I know, in history, poetry, or fiction; and when they had been slaughtered on the beach we contributed their heads, hearts, livers, and other less desirable organs to the people of the village, who were genuinely glad to get them. Meat is not often on their bill of fare.

French colonial administration, like that of other nations, may leave some things to be desired. But one thing whose value is incontestable the French have done for the Marquesans. They have built trails. As we entered the Bay of Virgins and were recovering a little from what was almost the physical shock of its prodigious beauty, some of us noticed, high on a hill so steep that it amounted to a grass-clad precipice, the zigzag of a trail climbing almost vertically above us, where it seemed as if no trail could possibly climb.

I remember saying, "There is one place you won't find me". But the call of the mountain was too strong for my laziness. Two days later I went. Or it may have been nothing but shame, for Mrs. Pinchot and Professor Pilsbry had climbed that ladder the day before.

So the next morning the Professor and I set out. We landed through the surf on the little beach, walked through the village along its narrow rock-bordered single street, lined at intervals with neat little houses raised on posts, and shaded throughout with coconut palms and breadfruit trees; passed the little Catholic church, boarded and painted and steepled; passed the diminutive Protestant church, with its coconut leaf walls and coconut leaf roof, and no steeple at all; passed the house of the Chief's father-in-law, where two were sick; passed the house where a victim of tuberculosis lay dying; passed the houses of many other sufferers; crossed on stepping stones the Hanavave stream of gloriously clear water; crossed a tributary brook over a bridge built by the French; passed the stone Virgins, too colossal to be recognizable as such nearby; and then on through the gorge beyond the town into the wider valley above, with its thousands of coconut trees; through a little strip of dense damp virgin forest; and out on to the open grasslands we had seen so plainly from the ship.

Then we began to climb, and as we climbed the great pillars and faces of volcanic rock began to take on their huge true values, and Hanavave Valley to show us what it had to show. At a corner of the trail we could not choose but sit and look and let the glory of the view sink in.

Directly underneath us was the village, but as completely hidden as the street below from a man who looks through the glass of a skyscraper window. To our left lay a little slice of harbor, its luminous water changing from green to blue as the depth increased. The ship was still concealed by the steepness of the hill.

In front of us and to the right lay the great valley, shut in by a noble rampart two thousand feet in height, up to which rose slopes too precipitous for even the avid vegetation of the tropics to overgrow them.

Directly below us stood out the great pillars of the more inland Virgins, the head of one of which, by an irony almost too great to be an accident, was changed at this height into a perfect reproduction of the head of that representative Protestant, William E. Gladstone, as drawn a thousand times in the *London Punch*. It was just the note of comic relief needed to humanize a landscape otherwise too impressive to be assimilated.

To the right, over against the harbor, the bounding ridge rose in a saw-toothed arête so thin and sharp that at least a hundred feet below the top it could be and actually was pierced through from side to side by an opening which showed to us as a large and vivid spot of light.

It seemed impossible, but there was no disputing it. Even among these islands, where one may see half a dozen natural bridges in half a dozen miles, this was no less than marvelous. We saw it and looked through it later from the other side as our schooner sailed around the island on the way back to Hiva Oa.

Here and there below us was the tiny hut of a copramaker, and everywhere throughout the less precipitous floor of the valley great groves of tall and slender cocoanuts, from which he and his like took the raw material of their simple living.

High on one slope lay an outcrop of bare brown lava with the faintest trace of a trail running across it. Another slope, so far below that it looked nearly level from where we sat, had been burned off by the escape of one of the fires copra-makers are constantly lighting to dispose of the rubbish which otherwise would make their work impossible. When a leaf, like that of the coconut palm, is fifteen or twenty feet long, six or eight feet wide, and weighs teens of pounds, it takes but a few of them to clutter up the ground.

As we sat drinking in the immeasurable beauty of this great scene, this carved and colored bowl of atmosphere into which we looked, further details began to emerge. Here the smoke of a copra-maker's fire, there a bit of clearing, and finally white birds.

White birds soaring across the faces of the cliffs, some easily seen, some at what seemed an infinite distance, sailing, swooping, diving in what must surely be flying for the mere delight of being on the wing. We saw one fall in a great curving sweep that must have spanned a thousand feet, and we thought that these white birds added the supreme and final touch of beauty, grace, and life. Titanic wildness and sylvan peace, flown over by white birds—it seemed almost too much.

After a while we saw that the birds were not Fairy Terns but Tropic birds—the birds around which cluster more story and romance than any others in these seas, except the Albatross itself.

Then it was time to go on up again over the well-built trail in pursuit of the fugitive top. As every mountain climber will understand, time and again we saw ahead of us the point that was obviously the very summit; and time and again, when we reached it, there lay a higher summit beyond.

As we rounded one of these alluring but mendacious corners, there shone before us the great waterfall without which no valley in these islands is altogether perfect. This one hung in mid-valley, hundreds of feet in height, with a flow of water slender enough to lend grace to the precipice over which it fell, and to contrast inimitably with the dark gigantic cloud-capped peak behind it, which was the summit of the island.

We tried to talk about it; we tried to photograph it; we failed in both; but we have seen it, and we can never forget it.

When we tore ourselves away from what was somehow the prodigious and yet intimate sweep and beauty of the valley and began to consider nearer things, we found ourselves in a topography of rounded minor ridges and little canyons, so steeply cut that 45 degrees was a very moderate gradient among them, and covered with a smooth grey-brown velvet of little ferns. They were like the familiar maidenhair in stem and leaf, and as accurately uniform in height as if they had been clipped. They made the ridges seem as strokable as the fur of a kitten, and just as flowing in outline.

At home grass-clad and fern-clad slopes such as we had been walking through for hours would have meant but one thing, and here we found they meant it also—fire. It was amazing and incredible in this tropic island, where rains were constantly drawn like curtains across the faces of the precipices and over the sea, but it was true. The vegetation of the interior of Fatu Hiva was as definitely conditioned and controlled by forest fires as in any mountain park in Colorado.

We noticed first that the ferns themselves had been burned off in little patches along the trail. Then in wet places in the bottoms of steep little valleys appeared small pockets of the original forest, just as a thousand times at home I had seen similar pockets survive in similar places when the fires had taken all the rest.

Then came stretches of burned trees, Pandanus palms and others whose relationships I could not even guess, silvering many a ridge with their bleached branches and showing the unmistakable marks of fire nearer the ground. We had not walked a mile before the proof was as complete as it was unexpected.

We were still discussing the power and the ubiquity of forest fires when out of the corner of my eye I picked up two Marquesans on horseback rounding a corner of the trail. Here was a chance to learn the distance to Omoa, the village south of Hanavave to which the trail we were traveling ultimately led.

They were two youngsters with wreaths about their hats, and the horses they rode were good. One of them spoke little or no French; the other rather less. I asked the linguist how far we were in kilometers from Omoa, from which village they had just come. The question floored him completely. Then I changed to the simpler measure of hours.

Hours he could wrestle with. At first he said his village was one hour away. Then he reconsidered his verdict and made it three hours. Finally, that estimate also demanding revision, he settled down to split the difference and call it two.

It was still only the middle of the day, and on the two-hour basis we could reach Omoa easily by mid-afternoon. So the Professor and I decided to go on, and I wrote a note to Captain Brown, which the young man agreed to deliver, asking him to have the launch meet us at Omoa about four o'clock.

Then it occurred to me to check this Fatu Hivan estimate of distance by asking how far we were from Hanavave. With great promptness and positiveness the linguist declared we could make it in one hour, and under much questioning stuck bravely to it.

Since it had taken us three hours of hard walking to get where we were, that upset our applecart completely. The note to Captain Brown, written on a scrap of the paper which had wrapped our lunch, went back into my pocket, and we determined to choose the evils of the long trail back to Hanavave rather than fly to others that we knew not of.

The young men having departed, obviously much puzzled as to what could induce two grey-beard Americans to labor up these hills afoot, the Professor and I pushed on to the next corner ahead, from which we hoped to see Omoa and the great cliff which bounds it to the south.

Again we passed point after point on the trail which we vainly hoped would show them to us. But at long last we came to where we could look down into the Valley of Omoa, scarcely less superb than that of Hanavave, and even into the fringes of the town.

Directly in front of us the great peak lay hidden in the clouds. Beyond the village the thousand-foot cliff, with more pinnacles on its summit than a Queen Anne cottage (a shameful simile), rose straight up from the sea, with the huge swell of the Pacific breaking at its foot. We had seen it from the water, and we knew that across the face of it swung Frigate birds, Boobies, Tropic birds, and the delicately beautiful white Fairy Terns—the most characteristic flying things of the high islands of Polynesia.

Sitting in stillness before so great a spectacle we ate our sandwiches and raisins, and then, while I waited to photograph the peak if only the clouds would lift, the Professor dropped down the hill in search of land shells. I watched his progress by the shaking of the vegetation, and very soon dropped down myself to join him. At once he set me to work.

Here was a little palm tree with long slender leaves dotted on the under surface with minute and delicate land snails. Would I kindly collect them? I would, and gladly. But the first leaf I reached up for and pulled off, to gather its inhabitants more conveniently, added a new fact to my experience—the fact of a tree-climbing angle worm.

Now as a fisherman I am thoroughly familiar with angle worms. While I no longer use them myself, preferring the dry fly, I have no scorn for those who do. I have dug them by the quart, and I know where to find them. But this was the first time I had ever seen an angle worm up a tree.

In the axil of the leaf I had pulled off was a little pinch of humus, and in the humus an unquestionable angle worm perhaps two inches long, and a very lively one at that. I tried to collect him, but he fell into the foot-deep litter on the ground and was gone.

The next leaf, however, provided another, and the next still one more. After that arboreal angle worms were definitely added to the list of contradictions I have known.

Whether the small boys of Polynesia go climbing for angle worms I do not know. In any case, in testimony of the truth of this evident impossibility I offer the angle worm and Professor Henry A. Pilsbry, Curator of the Academy of Natural Sciences of Philadelphia, as witnesses beyond impeachment or contradiction.

Our tramp so far had been no less than gorgeous, but the walk back was one of the most excitingly beautiful of my life. The setting sun shot its level rays against precipice and rampart and glorified them. It changed the brown fern velvet on the nearer ridges into the warmest russet until they glowed like polished carnelians, but of a finer and more fiery hue. It made one wish he might grow large enough to pass his hand over them, as one loves to handle the smooth surfaces of rounded jades.

The sea, clear of all vapor, was misty and mysterious with the white reflections of the Trade Wind clouds, which gave it a depth and distance no sharp horizon can ever show.

The sunset itself was nothing less than violent—as sunsets in the tropics often are. Hidden behind masses of dark cloud the sun glared, like a burning eye, out of a narrow crevice, and above and beneath the cloud wrack drove great fan-like beams of light, blue upward and yellow downward, to the zenith and the ocean. We saw the sun, which sets in quietness in temperate climates, go down amid the semblance of a vast explosion.

When we turned our backs to the sunset for a moment and looked eastward, the beauty of the Valley of Hanavave in the level rays was simply unbelievable. I have no words to tell of it, or to describe the illumination of the titanic rampart which fringed it to the right and left. It was almost impossible to leave the contemplation of it long enough to watch our footing and keep from stumbling down one of the grassy slopes, so steep that there would have been no chance whatever for the most active man to stop himself, once started.

Although the dark in the tropics comes with many

gradual steps and by no means at one stride, The Ancient Mariner to the contrary notwithstanding, before long the light began to fade and darkness was almost on us. Moreover, we were getting hungry. And leg weary too, for we had been climbing up or down for six or seven hours, and trans-Pacific trips on schooners give a man small chance to keep his legs in trim.

So we pushed on as rapidly as possible, finding, as many other travelers have found, that miles passed over easily on starting were much harder for tired men to travel going back. At length we sighted the Bay and the Virgins. And then we came to Gladstone's head.

I know what I am about to write will sound incredible, but certainly it could not have been invented. The failing light had not only left the likeness as striking as before, but had perfected and completed the resemblance to a *Punch* cartoon by adding (wonderful to relate!) the perfect counterfeit presentment of the flaring white stand-up collar which few caricatures of the Great Commoner ever failed to show. Absurd, of course, but we had to believe our eyes.

At length we came down to the coconuts. At length we passed the bridge, slipped through the darkened village, and could just see the outline of the skiff that was waiting for us out beyond the surf. We got off safely to the ship, shed and replaced our well-soaked clothing, and sat down to supper. And that was the end of a perfect day.

A day of days—rather a day of years, of lives. Titanic wildness and sylvan peace, flown over by white birds.

Marlin at San Clemente

MEXICAN Joe was sitting in the middle of the skiff and I in the stern, both facing backward, as the launch towed us under the cliffs a hundred yards from shore. It was a late, still afternoon, with a glassy heave on the ocean as the great Pacific rollers came in around the end of San Clemente Island. The western horizon was hidden from us by high shouldering hills, whose brown slopes fell away to black rocks at the water level. North and east the haze hid from us the heights of Santa Catalina Island and the mainland of California. The time, the place, and the water were all just right.

We were trolling for marlin. Fifty feet of tow-line separated us from the launch, and fifty yards behind us my bait, a flying-fish, gleamed now and then through the side of a swell. We were fishing and hunting at the same time, for in such calm weather the marlin often swims at the surface, with the half of his crescent tail and sometimes the whole of his dorsal fin above the water. You may have all the excitement of stalking big game before you hook your fish.

Only the day before we had hunted a pair of this wonderful fish for four hours, carefully dragging our hooks across their line of travel over and over again. Each time the great fishes saw the bait they rushed for it together, and each time an agonizing thrill of indescribable anticipation swept through us. Every fisherman will know what I mean. But that was all. It was the wrong time of day, and they would not bite.

The next morning at sunrise I had found and followed, hooked, and after more than two hours of a lively difference of opinion had landed a marlin eight feet nine inches long. That fish broke water forty-eight times in the course of the fight, and in one of his rushes took two hundred yards of line straight into the depths of the San Clemente channel in spite of the best I could do. The strength and grace of outline, the beauty of coloring of the superb creature—the rose, the blue, the olive, and the pearl—I shall never forget; but I had taken him from a large launch. I wanted to try now what sort of weather we should make of a similar fight from an ordinary fourteen-foot flat-bottomed skiff.

So on the evening of the same day we went at it again. Down the coast to the eastern end of the island we ran, and near the Hook sighted the fin and tail that forecast the best fishing, so far as my experience goes, the red gods have yet vouchsafed to mortals. But that particular specimen, wiser than he should have been at that time of the day, refused the bait, swam directly up to the skiff, looked at us, and departed.

Fifteen minutes later I had a strike. Joe cast loose from the launch and seized the oars. I struck with all my might, but the huge fish, hooked, as we saw later, in the bony side of the jaw, paid no attention. Joe backed water, I reeled rapidly, and we were within fifty feet of the marlin before he discovered what was wrong.

Then out of the deep he came. Then rush followed rush, leap followed leap. High out of water sprang this splendid creature, then lunged with his lance along the surface, his big eye staring as he rose, till the impression of beauty and lithe power was enough to make a man's heart sing within him. It was a moment to be remembered for a lifetime.

Then, the first fury over, the great fish started away. As rapidly as a man could row he towed our skiff a mile straight down the coast.

As soon as the marlin showed himself after the strike, the launch was sent back to camp for Dr. Chas. F. Holder, who knows more of big game fishing at sea than all the rest of us put together. But Dr. Holder had never happened to take a marlin or to see one taken. Indeed, I doubt whether two dozen all told have been caught in the history of angling in Catalina waters. So the launch disappeared in the failing light, and scarcely had it done so when our sea-horse turned and towed us out to sea.

The utmost efforts of Joe with the oars and myself with the rod barely sufficed to keep us within reasonable distance of the rushing fish. Darkness was falling fast, and by the time we were three miles out in the channel I confess to many a wish and many a look for the launch. Sunset was gone when it came. Joe, wisest of old sea dogs, had been lighting matches behind my back and holding them in his circling hands for the launch to see, and so it found us.

The tide was running strong, the wind rising against it, and the sea picking up. I welcomed Dr. Holder's arrival with distinct satisfaction. Afterwards Joe asked me whether I had been nervous. I gave myself the benefit of the doubt, and told him "No, because the launch was with us after dark." "Well," said Joe, "the skiff would have stood a great deal more sea than the launch. The only think I was afraid of was that the machinery of the launch would break down and the current carry her on the rocks at the Hook. We could always get in with the skiff, if a fog didn't come up."

Straight into the rising sea went the marlin, and there was nothing to do but follow him. For a time the crescent

Mexican Joe and the Marlin that Towed Us Seven Miles

Don't You Think Both Man and Fish Look Stuffed

moon shone thinly over the dim shape of the island, then moon and island disappeared together, while the great fish, with a strength I could neither break nor check, dragged the boat against wind and sea.

An hour went by, and then another, yet our motive power apparently was as strong as ever. By this time the sea was so high, as Holder told us afterward, that at times he could not see us between the waves. It was almost pitch dark, too, so that more than once, in the effort to keep close by, he nearly ran us down.

At last the steady strain began to do its work. The boat was gaining on the fish. I could not see, but I could tell. My line was doubled back for a few feet from the hook, and at last I felt the doubled part slide over the guide at the top of my rod. But the end was not yet.

Over and over again I brought the fish in with a steady pull, leaning backward against the rod until my body was horizontal and Joe, just behind me, could no longer use the oars. And as often as the doubled line came in, the fish saw the boat and made a new rush I could do nothing to control. Once he came between the blade of an oar and the boat, so that Joe struck him as he dipped. Yet we could not see him. More than once I was afraid the line would foul the launch as it crept up, and we yelled at it with all our strength to keep away.

Another half-hour passed, and the fish was getting tired. So, I admit, was I. But I doubt whether the stimulus of self-respect and the dread of failure were as strong in the fish as they were in me. A realizing sense of what it would mean to lose that fish kept me up to the work; and Joe's masterful handling of the skiff weighed heavily in favor of the rod and the fisherman. So when this great fighter was brought alongside for perhaps the twentieth time, still swimming upright, Joe managed to see him and gaff him near the head. But he was still a long way from being landed.

One hand still holding the rod, thumb on brake, with the other I managed to pass over the tail a slip-noose which Joe had made ready. The very instant it was done the launch ran into us, struck the skiff a resounding blow on the quarter, and the gaff slipped out.

You may have seen a cowboy sliding across a corral on his feet, one end of his riata round his hips and the other round the neck of a struggling bronch. Such an attitude seemed to me appropriate under the circumstances, and as I threw the rope behind my back it was clear to me that if the marlin got away he would have to take me with him. That fish was mine, for I had earned him.

But there was to be no such watery end to this particular fishing. It appears that the motive power of fishes resides principally in their tails, and the tail of this one was in my possession. The other end of him was speedily gaffed again, and then with a strong heave we slid the great and beautiful creature into the boat as a wave passed under us. There we lashed him, from the point of his sword to the root of his tail, with all the rope we had, and the war was over.

Two hours and thirty-five minutes; nine feet, three and a half inches; and one hundred and eighty-six pounds. Today he hangs upon my wall, with his mate of the morning, for a remembrance of the best day's fishing I have seen.

There had been seven marlin taken already at Catalina during the summer. My morning and evening fish made nine. But that was not all my luck, for between the two lost to themselves but saved to me a third saved itself

Dr. Holder Sits Down on His Bed

by the most remarkable rush in my experience of big game fishes.

This fish we saw on the surface at a distance, at about eleven in the morning. When the bait came within its line of sight there was a rush like an arrow, but the strike, as with the other marlin hooked that day, was steady and quiet. When I struck, the line was snatched from the reel with inconceivable rapidity. With very little pressure on the brake, the new twenty-four-thread line was actually broken against the water.

This statement will be incredible (until explained) to any man who has not taken heavy fish with light tackle. Most men who had will remember occasions when the reel had lost a hundred or a hundred and fifty yards of line, and the angler was letting it go with only the pressure absolutely necessary to prevent over-running, and all seemed well; when a sudden and suspicious slackness brought his heart into his throat, and after much hoping against hope the frazzled end of a broken line came gloomily in.

That was because the fish had turned at an angle to his former course, the line was forced to follow sidewise through the water in a sort of curved hypotenuse, joining the two sides of a triangle along which the fish was swimming, and then the pressure of the water broke it. So with my third marlin of this day, which I shall always recall and honor for that great rush.

A good many men have asked me whether the gentler kinds of angling still hold their charm after such big sea fishing as I have been trying to describe. My answer is, Emphatically, yes. I have taken also tarpon, kingfish, yellowtail, the Eastern jewfish, and the Western black sea bass, the albacore, and many kinds of shark, but in spite of it all I can still watch a float in a pond with the same pleasure, if not with the same thrill, as when I was a boy.

To catch half a dozen trout through a long late afternoon gives me the same deep satisfaction it always has. From the days when I angled for minnows with a pin, the delights of the running brooks have held me with a gentle firmness from which I have not escaped and never shall. One kind of fishing may be better than another, yet all are good. For me there is no answer to the question: "What would you rather do than go a-fishing?"

What Would You Rather Do?

FISHING is the one recreation which most nearly fits the needs of men from the cradle to the grave. The barefoot urchin with the thread and bent pin is the ancestor of descendants extending in an unbroken line to the old man, decrepit and world-weary, who yet is unable to answer the question, What would you rather do than go a-fishing?

Why is it that fishing holds this unique power over the sons of Adam? Wherein lies the charm of fishing? I do not know, although few feel that charm more vividly than I.

The extension of a man's personality into the strange world under the water may explain it in part, just as the power to affect great results at a distance is part of the charm by which the rifle holds the rifleman in thrall. The fisherman puts his hook, if not his hand, into a realm in which he cannot live, and exercises mastery there. It is an expansion of influence and power, and the charm of that is universal. Also, to catch a big fish on a small bait is very close to getting something for nothing, and the charm of that is more compelling still.

Then there is the mystery and uncertainty of fishing, the surprise and variety of it, the spice of chance and luck,—which attracts and holds like the spice of danger,— the endless differences between two days or two hours in the same boat at the same spot, or on the bank of the same stream and the same pool. Men love some things that are fixed and certain, but even more they love some things that are uncertain and not to be foretold, and there is nothing more so than the way fish do or do not bite.

No occupation can hold a man that does not absorb him. Fishing can and does. There is no separation from all the world beside so complete as that of the fisherman while he is fishing. It is not merely the lure of the fishing, but even more the quiet beauty of still waters, the downright vigor of the tumbling trout stream, and the unnumbered laughter and marvelous color of the sea. Fishing is more than its surroundings, but there is no delight in it more powerful than that of the places and conditions under which it can be followed by those who are fortunate enough to be its slaves.

Fishing, too, is an art not to be acquired in a day, and not to be pursued to the uniform satisfaction of its followers. Good luck is good only in contrast with bad luck. If the bite always followed the bait there would be little joy in fishing.

Fishing again is a perfectible art, in which nevertheless no man is ever perfect. Until the days come when desire shall fail, and the grasshopper shall be a burden, each year may see the fisherman more enviable in knowledge, more exquisite in skill, and so more capable of pure delight in fishing.

What other sport is so rich in pleasant tools and cheerful competition? The variety of tackle, some of which holds almost as potent a sway over the mind of the fisherman as the fishing itself, the test of wits and skill between the air breather and the water breather before the bite, the difficulties to be overcome in presenting the bait to the fish, are major parts of its enchantment.

But best of all is the fight with the fish itself when all

that goes before has been well done. I can remember, and so can every fisherman, struggles with hooked fish, the thrill of which after many years is still vital, and the triumph or defeat still almost as keenly felt as at the time.

Then there is the feeling of accomplishment, the right and the power of self-congratulation which follows the well handled taking of a good fish. You can hire men to chop down trees for less money than other similar labor commands in the same neighborhood because the man who chops trees sees accomplished before him from moment to moment the object of his labor, and is willing to take part of his pay in personal satisfaction.

So the man who has fought a fair fight, who has carried through to a successful conclusion the test of wits and the contest of nerve and skill, who has taken his fish with fair tackle in fair chase, has a right to feel proud; and so far as my experience goes that right seldom or never goes hidden or unexercised.

What lover of the angle can forget the beauty, or the strangeness, or the size, or the deliciousness of the big fish that did not get away? Walton is but the first of a long series of anglers to treat their catch as if they loved it. Good fishermen do. The men who kill no fish they cannot use are with us in greater numbers day by day. Of all the sports of capture, fishing is the most merciful. There is no need to kill unless you choose. The fish that gets away lives to be hooked another day.

On the conscience of the fisherman then are no wounded ducks, no paunch-shot deer. You catch your fish; if you don't want him back he goes, none the worse for his strenuous exercise.

At this point it is at times a comforting reflection that without conflict there can be no perfection. And if by chance now and again a released tarpon is taken by a shark, it is always open to the angler to square his account by the elimination of a few of these tiger-buzzards of the sea.

From one sin I may boast I have so far been free. No shark has ever struck my hook and got away alive with my consent. I have acquired merit upon many of them, and I thirst for yet more merit by the same road.

Pity the man who has no recreation, and pity, too, the man who does not number among the resources of his advancing years the gentle and stirring, the enthralling and yet quieting sport of fishing, the lifter of burdens, the restorer of power, the recreation not only of the contemplative man, but above all of the man who has work to do, and who needs to forget it for a time in order to do it well.

But with all the endless charm of fishing, there is one essential condition of its true enjoyment. Be not too anxious to fill your basket or your boat. The first and ostensible object of fishing is indeed to catch fish, but it is only the first. There is far more. Unless you can fish with serenity, unless you can be happy with few fish, unless there is a deep and true satisfaction in the fishing itself, unless you are willing to take thankfully what the Red Gods send, whether it be little or much, you cannot really love fishing, and you will not continue to love it to the end of your days.

Good luck is by no means the whole of fishing. But precisely wherein lies the power of its unfading charm I know no more than the day I caught my first trout.

Cod Liver Oil

WAS it your Father who took you fishing the first time you wet a hook? And do you owe him your initiation into old Walton's Brotherhood of the Angle? If he did, and you do, shake!

Both my Father and my Mother stood by while I landed my first fish—a native trout—a Pike County trout. That means a lot to me. And the story I am about to tell happened only because my Father took me with him.

It isn't such a much of a story, or anyhow the chances are it won't be to you. But to me it opened up paths of solid satisfaction and delight I have been following ever since.

Every boy has a great adventure, a first great adventure, which he remembers all his life. Mine came at Nantucket, that foremost whaling port of early American history, when I was a long-legged youngster of ten. I remember it as if it had happened yesterday.

We Pinchots boarded that summer with Captain Folger, one of the long succession of ship captains of that name, in an old-fashioned house about the middle of a steep cobblestoned street, up which the town crier came to ring his bell and cry "Fresh Swordfish". I remember well with what a shock I heard him cry one day that a man had been drowned in the harbor, and that his body still weltered to the parching wind, as the said crier might have put it if Milton had been within his cosmos, which he wasn't. Nor in mine either.

Across the street was a little shop in which I did my lessons, and worked over the insects I was collecting, and fussed with the bow and blunt arrow Captain Folger made me, and tried to make another arrow when a boil on my knee-cap kept me from roaming abroad.

Many of the Nantucket houses had railed-in lookouts on the roof for the delectation of retired sea captains, who could not break themselves of the habit of walking the quarter deck and scanning the sea. Also they contained, some of them, wonderful collections of scrimshaw—carvings of whalebone and whaletooth and walrus ivory, weapons and paddles from the South Seas, and curios from all over the world.

There were whale-ships at times in the harbor, but I was too young to grasp the romance and the mystery of whaling, to say nothing of its hardships and squalor, all of which Melville and Bullen opened to me afterwards. The weapons and the carvings, however, were well within my limitations. My Father bought me out of one collection a walrus tusk and a sperm whale tooth. I have them yet, both of them, and I wouldn't part with them for a horse and cart and a yellow dog under the wagon.

All this, however, is but the necessary setting and prelude to my first adventure.

Those were the days before the gasoline launch had made it easy and unpleasant to go anywhere by water. There was no hurry. There was no time-table, either, when we went pleasuring by sea. We were still at the mercy of the winds of Heaven, and quite content to be so.

So one day we took a cat boat, the whole Pinchot family, and sailed away in it. With us were the Reverend Doctor Bartlett, a fore-runner of that modern race of ministers who behave like anybody else, and my Father's friend Jim War-

The Town Crier

ren, kindest of companions even to a youngster like me.

Our expedition crossed the harbor in due season from Nantucket to the Wawinnett House, and landed for the day. Mr. Warren acquired glory in the uninstructed eyes of the inn keeper by registering as General Warren of Bunker Hill, was accepted as such, and treated as the General deserved. At the time the joke was beyond me, but not so his favorite song, whose chorus ran:

"For his spirit was treemenjous,
And fierce to behold,
For a young man bred a carpenteer
Only nineteen years old."

The Wawinnett House was famous then, and may be famous yet, for soft shell clams. I haven't been back to see. The rule was to eat until you could just see over the shells. At least one of us scrupulously observed that rule.

So noble a feed would have made a red-letter day for any small boy in the stage when Stomach is King. But the clams and the sweet corn were merely introductory. The next course was fish—tons of it.

On the narrow sandspit at Wawinnet two or three whaleboats were drawn up on the beach. In this degenerate day they wouldn't have been whaleboats, but of some lesser breed. One of them was launched through the little breakers of the quiet sea. We clambered in, rowed out a little way, but not beyond hailing distance from the land, and there we anchored. And then my adventure began.

This was no harbor we were fishing in, but the open sea. That was something for a youngster of ten. And not only were we fishing in the open sea, but we were fishing for sharks! Gee whiz! That was enough to set any boy on fire from head to foot.

And then the huge steel hooks! And the heavy lines!

And the iron chains between to keep the sharks from biting off the ropes! Shivers ran up and down my immature spine in quick succession.

Another wonder. The hooks were baited with little perch, a half dozen of them to each hook; perch caught in the fresh water pond near by; and every perch was slit down the back to make it easy to thread him on the enormous hook.

The lines were baited and thrown over. I was all a-quiver, though not allowed to fish, but only to sit and watch the others. But that was enough, and I didn't sit quiet for long. It wasn't possible.

Almost at once somebody got a bite. The line went taut, the shark was hooked. Gee whiz again! I was all over the boat and very much in the way, but of course I didn't notice it. All the world beside was blotted out.

Two or three men tailed on to the line and heaved together. Far down in the water something was fighting hard. The men pulled and the shark pulled. He made the line hiss through the water—I heard it. And he made a vast swirl before I saw him at all.

Then of a sudden the great deep was broken up. The shark burst into sight, the most tremendous and exciting object I had ever seen. Gee whiz! The whole end of him was just one great white mouth, wide open, with long slim teeth sticking up all round it, and the hook in one corner. It looked as big as the end of a barrel.

The slashing tail drenched us with spray, the head slammed back and forth, jerking the rope hard, the whole shark banged against the boat, the general welter and smother were beyond description, and I went almost wild with joyous excitement. It all amounted to a whale of a big time in the life of a little boy.

The skipper of the whaleboat wasted no time. He cramped the iron chain short across the gunwale, held the shark easily with one hand (I'll never forget that), and with the other beat him on the nose with a short wooden club till the subsequent proceedings interested him no more.

Then that shark was hauled into the boat with short-handled cargo hooks, like so much freight, and piled athwartship, while I hovered around in a frenzy of delight. I couldn't keep my hands off him, in spite of orders, but I had sense enough to stay away from that awful mouth.

Pretty soon up came another shark, with gaping, snapping jaws, teeth like a hedge, and a tail that was as good as a shower-bath. Once more the chain was cramped, the club beat down, the cargo hooks yanked in their prey, and I almost went into hysterics—all over again. And after that one more and more. It was altogether too good to be true.

And then I was allowed to hold a line myself! And I not only held the line, but I actually hooked a shark! Yes, I, me, myself, and undertook to haul it up to the boat, and got it nearly up there, too. It was as long as a man, and of course I was far too little to handle it. But I never asked for help. I got it, however, and promptly, just the same.

After a couple of crowded hours of glorious life that I wouldn't have swapped for anything I can imagine, two piles of clean-skinned gray-brown shovel-nosed sharks rose amidships above the gunwale. Being good and dead, or dead and good, I could make closer acquaintance.

In spite of warnings, I poked the wicked-looking eyes with their vertical slits of pupils; I rubbed my hands over the sandpaper which seemed to clothe the long slim bodies; I ran my finger along the edges and over the points of the long sharp teeth, and marvelled at the rows upon rows of them in the wide jaws, two of which hang on my wall this very moment. From that day on I was, and am, shark-minded.

All hands and the cook are interested generally in sharks, but I was furiously interested. I review the thrills of that afternoon whenever I come to grips, on rod, handline, or harpoon, with one of these incarnate appetites, whether it is no more than a harmless sand shark, like the Wawinnett scavengers, or a tiger shark with a chip on his shoulder. And have I had fun with sharks in the sixty years since then! I'm telling you.

We caught in all that day thirteen fish, which is perhaps one reason why ever since thirteen has been my lucky number. The largest of them was either eight feet two-and a half inches or nine feet two-and-a-half inches long. I helped to measure them, although I can't remember which. But even a shark ought to have the benefit of the doubt.

(The extreme scrupulosity shown in the last sentence will, it is confidently believed, inspire confidence in any statements which might seem to require support in other parts of this book.)

What a day it was! What a day of days! Take it for all in all, I shall not look upon its like again. And I owe it all to my fisherman Father's willingness to be hampered in his fishing for the sake of his small boy. For I took no small amount of looking after.

I shall never cease to be grateful that he took me with him in that whaleboat. It would have been so natural to leave the youngster behind, safely on shore with his Mother. That would have been the easy way. Sharks are no respecters of youth. Nobody could deny that.

But he took me with him just the same. And because

he did, a great experience lifted me out of the common round—not only that day, not once alone, but every time I catch a shark, every time I recall the story, and even now when I come to write it down.

And because my Father took me along, an interest was created in my life that has made it sensibly richer up to this very minute, and from which no one has suffered but the sharks. I will admit they've suffered a whole lot.

Fishing fathers will please take note. Fishing periodicals please copy.

When the whaleboat had no room for more sharks, and we were starting for the beach, I began to wonder what would be done with the great heaps of shark meat that filled our boat. Being from my youth a thrifty soul, I asked the skipper:

"What are you going to do with all these sharks?"

"We'll take the livers out of them," said he.

"Well," said I, "what do you want with the livers?"

"Oh," he said, "we use them for Cod Liver Oil."

And it might have been true at that.

Cape Lookout

WHEN you come to think of it, most fishing stories deal with the least interesting part of the fish population. They tell us about fish that have swum their race, that have fought their fight, that have been eliminated for good and all from any sport that you and I may ever hope to get. An uncaught fish gives us a chance, but the inanimate ichthys in the basket or the boat is a dead issue. He'll never be taken on any man's rod.

Nine out of every ten fish stories describe how your chance and mine has gone glimmering. But this story has to do with fish that are still in the sea. It opens in Doctor Russell J. Coles' houseboat in the bight of Cape Lookout on the coast of North Carolina, where I happened to be staying as an inquirer and a fisherman, and as his guest likewise.

Cape Lookout is a region different from any other I know, and its population of fishermen is a peculiar people. It lies upon an island, which is nothing remarkable for capes, but there is more to come. That part of the island which may be called the Cape embraces a square mile or two of sand where the houses of the little settlement defy the winds, and the sand is held in place by greensward. To seaward it is spread out in bare level stretches dotted with hillocks kept together by a rough beach grass. The long narrow point of the Cape is flat sand and nothing else.

Communication between the island and the mainland is maintained by the boats of the fish-buyers and over the wire of the life-saving station. There is no mail, or there was none when I knew it, which helped to give Cape Lookout its most unusual charm. In any sort of weather a postage stamp is a device of Eblis the Accursed. For details see *The Arabian Nights.*

The bight behind Cape Lookout has a glorious harbor deep enough for dreadnaughts, and landlocked to every wind that blows. From it have been reported by Doctor Coles more kinds of fish than have ever been found in any other spot in these United States, and many a species new to science also. Which is one reason why Cape Lookout has no near relations among places to go fishing. There is no spot I know of that has even a cousinly resemblance.

My friend Russell J. Coles is (now to my deep regret I must say was) without doubt the foremost American authority on the Dangerous Game of the Sea, under which title he could have written, he should have written, and I wish I could add that he did write one of the most fascinating of outdoor books. For he was not only a sportsman of unmatched experience, but an ichthyologist of international note, with decades of study and adventure to draw upon.

Doctor Coles was the man who took T. R. to Florida to harpoon a Manta, that prodigious flat-fish which reaches a breadth of somewhere between twenty and thirty feet from point to point of its gigantic wings. Doctor Coles told the President that, if he would make the trip to Florida, at a given place, on a certain day and date, he would show him Mantas.

The President kept the appointment. So did the Mantas, to the minute. And T. R., who was a hunter, but no fisherman, came, saw, conquered; hunted, harpooned, and took; one of these enormous examples of the big game of the sea.

Coles killed it with the spade lance he had invented for that purpose, after driving the boat squarely on top of the Manta, a proceeding calculated to interrupt the serene contemplation of nature in any mood.

Coles was a man of great physical dimensions, and corresponding physical power. For example:

The Cape is infested with tame cats gone wild. They feed on fish and reach about twice the normal size of household tabbies. When one of the largest Thomas cats crossed the gang-plank of his houseboat, Coles undertook to drive him out. The cat growled savagely, refused the open door, sprang upon the man, drove its long teeth through his right hand, and hung on like grim death to an Ethiopian.

Coles called to his boatman to hand him a knife, but the man was frightened and drew back. The cat bit and worried like a demon. It was up to the Doctor. He seized that grown up kitten behind the shoulders with his left hand, by the mere pressure of his fingers macerated the heart, and so killed the invader. Then he pried the clamped jaws loose, took time off to tell the boatman just what he thought of him, and proceeded to cauterize the wound himself. These beach cats are said to carry hydrophobia germs around as part of their regular equipment.

But Doctor Coles' specialty was not cats but sharks. They were almost a profession with the Doctor. And in a small way sharks are a hobby of mine, also. I have an appetite for sharks.

I was with the Doctor at Cape Lookout because I wanted to learn first-hand his method of harpooning and handling big sharks in the rough water of Cape Lookout Shoals. I was keen to check and correct my tenderfoot harpooning practice against his finished skill. I was a mere beginner,

Two Authorities on Dangerous Game — T. R. and Doctor Coles

with only a few tens of notches in my harpoon.

When school should have opened, however, the weather was bad. A southwest gale seemed to have been split in two lengthwise, so that what it lost in power it gained in duration. And it kept the water too thick and milky, and the sea too rough, for any chance to learn to use a harpoon.

But shark fishing was our purpose, whether with barbed harpoon or barbed hook. So we fished for sharks with a set line devised by Doctor Coles, the recipe for which is about as follows:

Take five whiskey kegs (empty if inside the three-mile limit) and a hundred yards of light steel chain. Attach kegs to chain at intervals. Sprinkle chain to taste with halibut hooks on steel wire snoods. Anchor each end with stout manila rope, season with whatever you happen to have for bait (skates for choice), set, and as the darky said to his hungry brother when he put the possum in the oven, "Come back when I calls you." The first man back gets the sharks.

We fished with fidelity, and not only with set lines, but with hand-lines, and with rod and reel. But gold is where you find it, and so is a shark—plentiful in prophecy, seldom as plentiful in fact, and often, when you want him most, not there at all. The muddy water that drove the food fish out to sea drove the sharks also, and the only notable result was what I take to be the world's record for the smallest shark ever captured on hook and line, a midget monster all of twelve inches long. I hold that record myself.

But while we waited for the southwester to blow itself out there was nothing approaching a dull moment. One day, for instance, while I sat on the smooth sand fishing in the twilight at the point of the Cape, there drew around me a living circle of big grey spirit crabs, each standing high upon his hairy legs, each with his eye-stalks at attention, each filled with a kind of threatening and dreadful curiosity.

With unhasting and unresting and almost imperceptible movement they drew gradually in. It was quite obvious they regarded me as food. There were enough of them to consume a man in no long time. It was gruesome beyond words. I am not used to being eaten alive.

Another day a great congregation of gulls skimmed low over and between the grassy hummocks of the Cape. They were behaving exactly like swallows in a field. What they were after I did not know, and neither did the Doctor, till his shot-gun proved to us they were picking grasshoppers out of the air, as they flew about on their private business. Which seemed all wrong for fish-eating sea-going gulls.

One bright day, but still no day to try the Shoals, we went out to see what we could see. One thing we saw was a great hammerhead who showed us his back fin, dawdled along his liquid road, and seemed to wait for our approach. He must have been a good twelve feet long. I was on tenter hooks, most eager to make sure of him. And that's exactly what I didn't.

I was in the bow, Coles and his captain watching me like hawks. My tendency is to throw too soon. It's just as bad to wait too long. And wait too long is what I did. The great fish sank, I threw as he was sinking, and away he went, with a great sweep of his tail to close the incident.

It's true that the hammerhead was right in the eye of the sun, but what's the good of an excuse? And it didn't help at all to know exactly what Coles and his men were thinking of me, though they said never a word.

We tried for sharks in the protected waters of Hobe Sound with chum and bait. A shark or two found the slick and followed it, quartering exactly like a bird dog on a scent, except that no bird dog ever could compare with a shark in olfactory keenness or equipment. But we took nothing.

While we waited and watched the shark fins cut diagonally up current through the slick till the scent faded, then turn and cross through it to the other edge, all the time getting nearer to the source of fish perfume, Doctor Coles told me the story of another great hammerhead that had his hangout (you couldn't say his home) in the quiet waters of Hobe Sound. This hammerhead had established a sort of modus vivendi with an ancient Hobe Sound fisherman, the terms of which appeared to have two articles: Item—The shark was not to bite the fisherman; and item again—the fisherman was to give the shark something to bite instead.

The ancient daily set his net and hauled it. To it came the shark, but not to use his teeth upon it, or his tail. Instead, he waited patiently outside the net for such unconsidered trifles of unmarketable fishes as the fisherman might choose to throw him. He never broke the net or hurt the man at all, although the old man stood and the great shark lay almost cheek by jowl in the shallow water.

Coles knew the man, and saw the hammerhead. Otherwise I would never have believed the story. The man has long since gone to his reward. I suppose the shark has also.

One breathless moonless night we tried a game I've never tried before or since—harpooning in the dark without a light. The launch carried us through the solid blackness in the still water behind the shelter of the Cape. The bay was glassy smooth and full of fish, and the water filled with the little living creatures which make phosphorescence when disturbed.

As we went streaks of fire darted away from our bow

like lines of molten spray. Each fish that fled into the darkness left a trail of light behind. It was a sight that kept me agape with wonder.

And every fish left his name behind him, written in living light as he darted off. One fish swam straight, another curved away, another zig-zagged in his flight, and where each went the fire of his passage remained behind. Each kind had an individual course that marked it from all the others. The captain of the launch could name them, every one.

Last of all, as we came slowly homeward, a great shark passed us in a blaze of phosphorescent light wider than our launch, and almost as long. I can not begin to make you see the impressiveness of that great halo which enwrapped and hid the fish as fully as Jove's famous cloud hid him, but far more beautifully. For this cloud was made of light, not darkness. I threw, which was perhaps ungrateful, and the shark went off unharmed, which was no more than his desert.

We tried the surf for channel bass, and caught but little. We tried for Mantas and smaller rays, but took not one. But we did see how the young ray begins his aqueous life full in the air—how his mother whirls like a cart wheel above the water, and in the course of it casts off her offspring. The newly born, with his wings folded about him, splashes into the sea, unfolds his wings, and from that moment paddles his own canoe.

Another day the water as we left the bight was gorgeous with shifting copper disks, reflections from the rising sun, each with its lighter border of color playing swiftly over the unruffled sea. It was a sight to drive a painter frantic.

Another day I watch the hauling of a seine, and in it a sea turtle and many fish. And yet again we fished in the offshore swell about the English tramp steamer, sunk with 8,000 bales of cotton ten years before, and were careful not to run upon the iron reef she made. Or we ran a net around a school of bluefish or Spanish mackerel. It was all in the open and all good.

By and by the southwester blew itself out, the weather began to clear, and the sea to fall. With that our hopes rose high. We were to use the harpoon on Lookout Shoals, which run southeastward from the Cape, as soon as it was possible for a boat to live there. Part of the Lookout Shoals are dry at the ebb, part are barely covered, and there is little water on them even at flood tide.

Off shore there had been heavy weather. On this particular day a ground swell six to ten feet high was rolling in from the southeast, curling about the spear point of the Cape, and breaking in from both sides, as is the nature of ocean swells.

Across the point ran another line of combers, so that the seas swept over the Shoals from three directions. They made a boiling witches' cauldron as the shouting rollers ran across the shallows and dashed against each other. Where they met they drove the spray thirty feet in air. It was such a welter of tumbling, broken, foaming water as it seemed to me no open boat could venture into and survive.

Our sturdy motor launch carried a small house forward, but was open for more than half her length. It looked like suicide to take her in. But since Coles had seen and done too much to throw his life away without good reason, and since two members of his crew had families at home, I figured that if they could stand it, I would have to.

According to orders, then, I took my place on the little forward deck, braced myself against the house, held the harpoon firmly in my two hands, so that the line ran clear, and prepared my mind for eventualities and a ducking.

The ducking left nothing to be desired in prompt delivery and full weight as the *Starlight* at half speed loafed through this incredible confusion of spouting breakers. Personally I have never seen anything like it, although I have had much boating in rough waters. The only reason we were not filled and sunk in two minutes was that, for some miraculous reason, when a sea broke that would have sunk us, and that was all the time and nearly everywhere, we were always somewhere else.

Just ahead of us the great combers would be covering acres with continuous foam. I in the bow would speculate: Do we turn away to starboard or to port? We can't go through them. And instead of port or starboard we would proceed straight into the very center of chaos, and be saved from disaster only because chaos was busy in another spot, and not a wave broke till we were past.

Broadside on, here came a comber toppling to its fall. If it broke against us it would fill us in a single second. It didn't. It merely lifted us ten feet into the air, and broke the instant it had passed us. Every half minute brought its separate miraculous escape.

Except that I knew Coles knew his business, and his men knew theirs, I would have bet the bulk of my inheritance that our boat could not have lived to travel fifty yards. Yet we wandered for an hour at a time through this leaping, clashing confusion of shifting cliffs and canyons, in the midst of which I just barely managed not to be jerked overboard; and we never shipped a sea. It was the perfection of surfmanship. I would not have believed it if I had not seen it myself.

"How do you do it?"

"Easy enough. Cross shallow places in the trough, and

never let a sea hit the boat square, either forward or aft. Take them all quartering."

Easy enough of course. Easy for Blondin to skip across Niagara on his tight rope. Easy enough for Jenny Lind, and Patti, and Caruso, and Lily Pons to enrapture the world with song. But passing wonderful to us who sit and watch or listen. So it was to me when the skipper not merely practised his simple rule (simple to him), but added to it his knowledge of what the seas would do, where they would break, and when. That amounted to divination.

As the great swells ran across the Shoals, smashed furiously together, and shot their geysers up against the sky, the *Starlight* jumped and rolled, was thrown up and banged down till the bottoms of my feet were sore, and pitched and twisted with motions as unpredictable as those of a bucking horse, and seemed to do her prettiest to throw me.

And very, very nearly did. And all the time, one of Coles' men was standing on top of the house without a wall to brace against, without a rope to cling to, and kept his balance on that plunging platform as easily as you and I would stand and look in a shop window.

I don't know whether I have made you see the picture, but the whole thing was exciting, exhilarating, enthralling to the last point. And these men handled big sharks in such waters! No wonder I was wild to see it done. But see it I did not, for not one large shark appeared in all the days we worked the Shoals.

My harpoon itched in my hands. I was as eager to throw as a boy is to fire the .22 he got for Christmas. Once a ladyfish, a ray six or seven feet across the wings, did give me a mark. I threw—and missed. It was my one and only chance on the Shoals, and I foozled it. Sic transit gloria mundi, if you know what I mean.

On still another day we tried the Diamond Shoals of Cape Lookout. Not the Diamond Shoals where the light-ship rides, and not named, I take it, for the diamond-back terrapin which abound in the creeks and inlets of this favored coast. Coles used to keep them in a barrel (the turtles, not the Shoals), feed them on crabs, and stew them with butter at the psychological moment. Nothing was ever better. But the Diamond Shoals were no more productive than the others, although they added to my experience an even fiercer sea.

And still another day just beyond the breakers we ran into acres of young menhaden—shad or fat-backs in the local tongue, moss-bunkers or bony fish off New York, and many another name besides. They were deep chested fish less than a foot in length, they swam in solid masses, crowded within three or four inches of each other, and their phalanx went deeper than we could see.

Where these uncountable multitudes swam, the whole aspect of the sea was changed. The action of numberless fins and tails overlaid the ocean with a fretwork of little ripples that traveled with them as if it were the clothing of the great school.

There were hundreds of thousands, or more probably millions, of fat-backs, and under them and through them swam the sharks, punctuating the progress of the school by the eruptions of their smashing strikes. They preyed incessantly on their smaller brothers, like magnates on the common people.

The dodging fish opened narrow lanes as the sharks drove through them. Sometimes, so thick they swam, the lanes were only two or three feet wide. And with each vicious strike hundreds of fat-backs sprang from the water in a sort of living spray, and fell back with a roar.

The enormous plethora of living things was prodigiously stimulating and impressive. Its fascination refused to fade as we drifted through the dense school over and over again.

For a shark it must have been paradise. As soon as his last meal had gone down so far that he could swallow again, all he had to do was to strike and fill himself once more to the very teeth. In his eagerness to do so a black-tip shark threw himself clear of the water, which is as fine testimony to the vigor of that vigorous fish as I can give, for he must have been loaded to the guards.

The sharks among the fat-backs were small. Now and again as one came near, I threw at him. The first four I missed narrowly. The fifth, a black-tip, the harpoon went clear through. In spite of that he made a fight beyond his inches, and did honor to his fiery race. He was four and a half feet long.

The sixth came toward us quartering, wedging apart the ranks of fat-backs as he came. He must have been six to eight feet below the surface, but almost straight under the boat, when the harpoon reached him. He also became attached to me, I pulled him in without ceremony, and he was five feet long. In these waters that was too small to count.

Twice a great tarpon rolled so near that his huge scales showed plainly. It was pleasant enough to know that he was about, but the masses of fat-backs dwarfed him and all the rest to insignificance. The big fish were mere incidents, these little myriads the central thing. As a saga of life without words the whole scene gripped me and held me and holds me still.

That which specifically I came to Lookout for, I never got. I got much else, but no great shark was impaled upon my iron or bled beneath my lance. They are all there yet, so far as I'm concerned, and still to be taken by you or by me.

This is no story of dead fishes. Live fish and better fish are still in the sea than hook and line have ever taken out of it.

Time Like an Ever Rolling Stream

MEN may come and men may go, but the Sawkill brook flows on—feeding its trout, protecting its insect, molluscan, and crustacean life—a home and a hiding place for myriads of living creatures—a thing of beauty and a joy forever.

Along its banks giant Pines and Hemlocks have germinated and grown, flourished and died, decayed and vanished, uncounted generations of them, each leaving its contribution to the richness and glory of the place—and in their branches other uncounted generations of squirrels and birds have fed and quarreled and mated and carried on the business of their world.

Under the shade of little needles on great limbs deer and bear drank and listened as they drank. About their roots cubs, fawns, and baby otters romped and rested and romped again. In winter their cones and leaves strewed the snow after every breeze, and on sunny days melted little cavities for themselves, and froze there as the shadows fell across them.

Buffalo, moose, elk, wolves, and panthers left their tracks beside the semi-human tracks of bears and coons, the webbed tracks of beaver, and the triangular imprints of mink.

Great flocks of passenger pigeons hid the sun, and where they settled the branches of stout trees were broken off and crashed to earth, to the thunder of innumerable wings.

Kingfishers clattered up and down the gorge in high water and low, as through the years the weather and the water shaped the rocks and the floods ground out great potholes with their in-arching rims.

Century upon century of milleniums passed over the Sawkill and left it very much as they found it. At times great Pines and Hemlocks fell across the stream, at times the rush of the torrent after great rains moved them away to new positions, to be moved again or to disintegrate where they lay by the slow action of the elements.

Now and again a sandbar changed its place, a pool was deepened by a fall of rock or shallowed by the cutting of a new channel. Great trout grew fat and lazy in the slow current of beaver dams, and the full-fed water snakes sunned themselves where countless forebears had coiled in comfort before them.

When the redmen came, the life of the brook changed, but only a little. For they were no slaughterers, but conservationists, blood and bone, and took no more than the natural increase. Each family had its hunting grounds in which no other family might hunt except for food while passing through, and the penalty for breaking that game law was sometimes death.

Now and again through the centuries a forest fire set by lightning swept one or the other bank, or maybe both, and changed the lives of land and water dwellers for a few or many generations.

For uncounted ages the redmen hunted on the Sawkill, and still the greater and the lesser tribes of wood and stream lived with them, not one destroyed, not one dangerously reduced in numbers by anything the Indians did. Then came the change.

White men appeared. With new weapons of destruction,

At Ten Giff Cast a Workmanlike Fly

In the Spring the Angler's Fancy Lightly Turns to
Thoughts of Trout

new zeal for slaughter, new appetite for conquest, they made new demands on nature for the means to live a new kind of life. With their coming the axe began to modify the face of the earth, and the days of the wilderness were numbered.

The slow and uneventful march of the centuries over the Sawkill changed almost over night to the rush of oncoming civilization. The old order, grown out of thousands of generations of adjustment, and the old balance, painfully won through the life and death and internecine struggles of myriad forms of life, suddenly found themselves powerless before a new and strange attack, against which they had no time to develop a method of resistance.

The Indians gave way before it, and disappeared. The buffalo, the elk, and the panther followed them. The primeval forests went down before the need for houses and ten thousand other needs for wood. The white man was reaping where he had not sown, and nature paid the price of the better living, the faster thinking, and the more stable existence of the heirs of all the ages.

Hemlocks that overhung the riffles and pools of the Sawkill when Columbus discovered America were still vigorous trees when the first Pinchot to set foot in Pennsylvania twitched his first trout out of the Sawkill, and found it good. With him came his son, a boy of nineteen, who the year before had been on his way to join Napoleon's army as a recruit when the battle of Waterloo put an end to his soldiering.

The son threw himself into the life of his new country with the vigor which distinguished him. The tribes of Pine and Hemlock along many streams paid him tribute, with the years much land passed into his keeping, and he prospered and grew strong, while the Sawkill hurried and tarried on its never-ending march to the sea.

His son, my Father, was born and grew up in the little village which occupied the level plain between the Sawkill and the Delaware, and in the days when artificial flies were yet unknown, became so skillful an angler with more natural bait that few fly fishermen I have known could match him.

I in my turn became a lover of the Sawkill and its sister little rivers, and under my Father's eye I learned the uses of the worm. I took full many a trout with it, and in due and early season graduated to the wet fly and the dry.

But my best performance with any fly was far below the high craftmanship of my Father's handling of a worm.

When my son announced his participation in the affairs of this world by the barbaric yawp of infancy, his Mother and I destined him to be a fisherman. Anxiously we waited for the time when he might take his first trout, and take an interest in taking it. At the age of three, accordingly, we explained to him about fishing, which dissertation he obviously failed to comprehend, and asked him if he wouldn't like to catch a tiny speckled little trout.

Being, like other youngsters, ready to try anything once, he assented—and the cortege moved in solemn procession to the stream. It was no light matter. The son and heir was about to begin his career—catch his first fish.

So I hooked a trout, handed Giff the rod, and urged him to pull. He pulled; the trout struggled on the bank; and the boy, casting an indifferent eye on what should have engaged his whole I. Q., passed on with no interval whatever to matters of greater juvenile interest.

What a shock was there, my countrymen! Rubia and I were struck with horror. I couldn't be consoled even by the fact that I had just taken several trout on a leader made by myself out of a knotted succession of single strands of

Rubia's hair. Was it possible that the son of such parents could fail to love to fish? We couldn't believe it, and, what was more, we didn't intend to stand it.

And we didn't have to. We let nature take its course, and, because we did not press him, before he was ten Giff was casting a workmanlike fly. From then to now on more than one occasion he has brought back more trout than his instructor and progenitor. And he loves to fish about as much as I do.

"Dad," said the fifth generation of Pennsylvania Pinchots on a day when everything was right, "how about fishing this afternoon?"

"I thought I would," said I.

"Hot dog!" replied this worthy son of a slang-infested father. "What rod you goin' to take?"

"Well, I thought I'd take the two-and-three-eighths-ounce Leonard. There's too much wind for the one-and-three-quarters."

"What fly you goin' to use?"

"A spider," said I.

"Hot dog!", said Giff again, out of the limited objurgatory vocabulary of youth.

So father and son settled the preliminary details, and when four o'clock came off we went in the open car, up over the hill behind the house, past the little red Schocopee schoolhouse where Rubia and I cast our votes at every election, to the brook I have been fishing for more than fifty years.

There we put our rods together, first carefully anointing the ferrules by rubbing them on our noses, as good fishermen do. Then we chose white and brown spiders, with long hackles and little hooks, out of my horn snuff box, with Napoleon's tomb carved in relief on the cover; made sure that the barbs had been broken off with a pair of sharpnosed plyers (we never fish for trout with barbed hooks any more); tied leaders to spiders with the Turle Knot; and oiled the hackles of our spiders with three parts of albolene to one of kerosene. Then the war was on.

It was a good war, and a swift. Before you could say Jack Robinson, Giff had a nine-inch native. Untouched by human hand, back into the stream he went, thanks to the debarbed hook, with nothing but a little healthful exercise to remember his adventure by. I always get great satisfaction out of that.

Then no more rises for a while, until, as the sun sank low, thick and fast they came at last—the little to swim away unhurt, and the less little to drop into the creel after they had been put to sleep with the back of a jack-knife. We had all we wanted long before it was time to quit. So we sat down on a log and held a session on the State of the Union.

"Dad, how long has this brook been here?", asked Giff, after long pondering.

So I told him, as best I could, and when we got home I tried to write it down. And that's what you've been reading.